W9-COT-848

Literature

Its Opponents and Its Power

Arther Trace

University Press of America, Inc.
Lanham • New York • London

Copyright © 1997 by
University Press of America,® Inc.
4720 Boston Way
Lanham, Maryland 20706

3 Henrietta Street
London, WC2E 8LU England

Library of Congress Cataloging-in-Publication Data

Trace, Arther S.
Literature : its opponents and its power / Arther Trace.
p.   cm.
Includes index.
l. Literature--History and criticism. I. Title.
PN524.T68 1996   809--dc20   96-43481 CIP

ISBN 0-7618-0589-3 (cloth: alk. ppr.)

Contents

Preface

Perhaps in no period since the Middle Ages has serious literature—specifically fiction, poetry, and the drama—been regarded less as a legitimate source of truth than in the past half century. As a result, its prestige, particularly in America, has plummeted, and in fact a multitude of powerful forces now so threaten it that it may well be on its way to becoming an inconsequential influence in American culture.

Even in the Middle Ages the enemies of literature were not so dangerous as they are now. Many medieval intellectuals regarded imaginative literature as a threat to society, especially because it has the power of arousing the emotions—the baser emotions, its enemies held—and therefore was to be looked upon with suspicion, if not alarm. In our time, on the other hand, the problem is not that it is considered a powerful threat to society but rather that it is irrelevant, and therefore not to be taken seriously.

In America it is becoming particularly evident that poetry doesn't sell, that serious plays are rarely performed, and therefore not published, and that serious fiction is gradually losing its audience. In most American schools the great literature is now largely neglected, as those who are closely familiar with the typical school curriculum well know, and in the universities many students are awarded degrees without ever having studied the literature of America or of the world. Academically, literature is approaching the status of a frill.

The first part of this study addresses four major kinds of threats which appear to be besieging the literary arts. The first of these describes in two chapters the intellectual revolution which has taken place over the past century and a half and which weakened the authority not only of literature but of the humanities in general, in favor of science and the scientific spirit. Or, put another way, this revolution replaced the authority of reason, the memory, and the imagination with the authority of the senses. Imaginative literature has thus been only one of the major casualties of this unprecedented intellectual development, but it is the one with which this study is mostly concerned. The second of these threats involves the literary theorists themselves, who, as I shall show, have, however inadvertently, been undermining the authority of literature by inventing theories which in fact trivialize it, and even threaten to destroy its authority utterly. In other words, the very intellectuals to whom the preservation of the prestige and rationale for the literary arts has been entrusted are in the process of annihilating them.

A third threat to the literary arts comes from the schools and colleges and universities. This threat takes two forms: first, American elementary schools, by virtue of unworkable methods of trying to teach students to read, have been turning out semi-literates by the millions, a phenomenon which is bound to exacerbate the decreasing role which literature has been playing in American culture. Second, the high schools and the colleges and universities are responsible not only for the gradual dissolution of the canon of the greatest literature, but in other ways, as I shall show, are preventing students from inheriting their literary heritage.

An even more serious threat perhaps because, unlike the other three, it is irreversible and still growing, is the enormous influence of audio-visual and electronic techniques of communication which in time may all but smother the written page in general and literature in particular.

Chapter V of this study challenges these prevailing anti-literary winds of doctrine by reaffirming the idea that literature is, as Sir Philip Sidney put it, "the highest form of earthly learning." It will assert that the *potential* power of literature has been not at all diminished from that assigned to it by literary theorists from the Renaissance through much of the 19th century. It will outline an essentially eclectic theory of literature which can be of use to those who know in their hearts that there is no substitute for the literary imagination and the power of literature but who have not been very successful themselves in articulating such a theory. The final chapter attempts to assess the prospects for literature in the future as its enemies close in. The Appendix lists in chronological order 102 representative declarations concerning the nature and purpose of literature from Plato to the present, and therefore furnishes a kind of gloss on some of the main points that this study makes.

Even in a book ten times the length of this one, such a task would be formidable, and it may be that no quantity of words, however well arranged, can persuade those who would trivialize or otherwise denigrate the beneficial capacities of literature. But one must start somewhere, and it is hoped that this study may do something to fortify the conviction of those who believe that the study of literature is one of the worthiest of occupations, and perhaps to make at least slightly uncomfortable those who are convinced that it is the most frivolous of occupations.

One final word: This study is rather lightly documented because even though it presents a multitude of facts, its primary aim is to evaluate those facts and to arrive at conclusions about the plight of the literary arts. Those who have a special affection for literature will, I hope, understand that I did not want to interrupt the flow of the discourse with heavy documentation.

Chapter I

The Triumph of Science
Over the Imagination

The prestige of literature during the course of the history of Western Civilization has had, one may say, its ups and downs. By "literature" I mean here primarily drama, poetry, and—when it finally came into its own—prose fiction. This chapter will examine briefly the heights and depths which the imagination, and hence the literary arts, have reached from Classical times to the end of the nineteenth century.

To summarize the whole story briefly, it may be said that Greek civilization regarded poetry and the drama with respect, even reverence, despite the warnings of some highly influential ascetic intellectuals like Plato. Even Roman civilization accorded literature a remarkable degree of prestige, although it was not much interested in the literary drama. With the advent of Christianity, however, during the Middle Ages especially, the literary arts fell upon hard times. Their prestige rose gradually again as the Renaissance progressed, and then climbed to their highest point in the hierarchy of learning during the later eighteenth century and the earlier nineteenth century. They began falling again toward the middle of the nineteenth century, particularly as the scientific method gained authority, until in the twentieth century, their prestige has sunk lower than at any time since the Middle Ages.

So blunt a summary requires serious qualifications, and there in fact may be some who do not even agree with this picture, particularly as I have viewed the condition of literature in the later twentieth century. But I should like to elaborate upon this summary with the aim of identifying the enemies and friends of the literary arts, the nature of their arguments, both pro and con, whose arguments prevailed when, and something of the ongoing controversy over the efficacy of literature during the periods when it was particularly sharp.

*****

Anyone who undertakes to defend literature as "the highest form of earthly learning," as Sir Philip Sidney expressed it, must also undertake to defend the supreme powers of the imagination; for literature, like the fine arts, is a product above all of the imagination. Historically, therefore, the fortunes of literature have been tied to the relative prestige of the imagination.

In general, it may be said that in ancient Greece the faculty of the imagination was regarded in some quarters even more highly than reason. No writer among the ancient Greeks was so revered as Homer. Even Plato was jealous of Homer, for in *The Republic* he warned against those eulogists of Homer who claimed that "he has been the educator of Hellas and that he is profitable for education and for the ordering of human things and that you should take him up again and again to get to know him and regulate your whole life according to him." True enough, Homer in *The Odyssey*, and especially in *The Iliad*, was writing about historical events, or supposed historical events, but he was writing about them in an imaginative way, in a way which produced the effect of immediacy, with dialogue and high drama and exalted language, and all the other techniques and embellishments that distinguish literature from history. Plato acknowledged that "there is an ancient quarrel between philosophy and poetry," but the very fact that such a quarrel existed indicates how highly the works of the imaginative writer were regarded, to the point, in fact, that they challenged the authority of the philosophers themselves, and sometimes seemed even to have won out.

Plato came to be known as the chief Greek enemy of the imagination in general and of poetry in particular. In *The Republic* he proposed some of the most enduring of arguments against literature. And the fact that he would not have poets in his ideal commonwealth (except those who praised the gods and famous men) was ever after known to both friends and enemies of literature, who felt that they had in one way or another to deal with his pronouncements.

It may be said that Plato offered two basic arguments against poetry: one was the metaphysical argument and the other the ethical argument. His insistence that poetry is thrice removed from reality is well known. There is less realty in a painting of a bed, he argued, than in the bed itself, and less reality in the bed itself than in the idea of a bed. Similarly, the imitation of a human action in a poem is more remote from the truth than the human action itself, and the human action is more remote than the idea of the human action. Thus, Plato concluded, poetry is too misleading to be a major source of truth. He argued too that poetry arouses the emotions of the audience in a way that interferes with their reason. The poet, he charges, "awakens and nourishes and strengthens the feelings and impairs the reason." And again, "Poetry feeds and waters the passions instead of drying them up; she lets them rule, although they ought to be controlled if mankind are ever to increase in happiness and virtue."

Thus the groundwork was laid for the next two thousand years and more for the controversy over the validity of the imagination, and hence of imaginative literature as a legitimate source of truth. Aristotle, by way of reply, wrote *The Poetics* in order to demonstrate that poetry is indeed a legitimate source of truth, that it is "a more philosophical and a higher thing than history," for poetry tends to express the universal and history the particular. In fact, Aristotle in *The Poetics* made himself perhaps the most influential and among the most powerful advocates of literature and the imagination in the Western World. He also argued for poetry on the grounds that its emotional appeal produces a purging effect which may be interpreted, though somewhat controversially, as producing a beneficial moral effect.

Similarly, Longinus contributed more than any other classical rhetorician to the realization of the power of language upon the emotions in his *Treatise on the Sublime,* in which he pointed out that "the effect of elevated language upon the audience is not persuasion but transport." And he emphasized the emotional power of elevated language more convincingly perhaps than any other classical rhetorician.

But as it turned out, the most influential literary theorist from the classical period was not Aristotle but Horace, who in *The Art of Poetry* defended literature in his own, if more desultory way. The key passage in *The Art of Poetry* is Horace's statement that "the aim of the poet is to inform or delight or to combine together, in what he says, both pleasure and applicability to life." The phrase "to inform and to delight" became known as the Horatian formula, and it was quoted by most defenders of literature from the Middle Ages on through most of the eighteenth century. The fact that Horace rather than Aristotle became the chief classical apologist for literature is due in part to the fact that Aristotle's *Poetics* was largely unknown throughout the Middle Ages and that he wrote in Greek rather than in Latin, which had become the *lingua franca* of the learned in Europe.

During the classical period, especially in Greece, the poet enjoyed a particularly high social station. He was commonly considered to be a seer, a prophet, and poetry itself to be of divine origin. The divinity of the poet was widely upheld, and the divinity of Homer exceeded them all. He was considered an authority on everything that he wrote about, often to the consternation of those who claimed that they were better authorities, everyone from military leaders to shipbuilders. Even in Rome, the poet enjoyed a special esteem, and the works of Virgil and Ovid and Horace seemed in Roman eyes to justify their privileged status.

But the exaltation of the poet and his role in society came to a gradual end with the advent of Christianity; for Christianity, for its own reasons, came to distrust the imagination and those who exercised it. The Church fathers were inclined to invoke Plato in their denunciation if it, and they discouraged the reading of the classical writers because they knew that classical poetry helped keep a pagan religion alive, even though—or perhaps because—they themselves were frequently well versed in it.

The Church was especially suspicious of the drama and of the theater. Church fathers like St. Chrysostom, St. Cyprian, Lactantius, and Salvian, all lashed out against the theater, widely regarding it as Satan's workshop. Tertullian's treatise *De Spectaculis* was perhaps the most devastating attack on theatrical activity during the Roman Empire. At any rate by the middle of the fifth century theatrical activity had disappeared entirely, and with it virtually all secular imaginative literature. In the late period of the Roman Empire it may be that Apulius's picaresque novel *The Golden Ass* was the only original secular work. Music and art suffered a similar fate in part because they too were expressions of the imagination, which the early Church had come so profoundly to distrust.

Gradually however the authority of the imagination was rescued by the Church itself. This phenomenon came about evidently from an attempt to assign more important meanings to certain passages in the Scriptures than the literal meaning signified, as, for example, in the more sensuous passages of *The Song of Songs*. In any case, allegorical interpretations, particularly of the Old Testament, became common in the early centuries of Christianity, and gave a new meaning, indeed a new power, to poetical passages in the Scriptures. Gradually the allegorizing of pagan classics became common. Fulgentius, for example, in the sixth century in a work called *Expositio Virgiliana* offered an allegorical interpretation of *The Aeneid* in which he attempted to demonstrate that what Virgil was really doing was telling a story of the progress of the human soul. However questionable such efforts may have been, they lent a new dignity and complexion to the literary imagination, and some Christian intellectuals began to perceive that the literary arts could be harnessed in the cause of religion.

Dante gave a new dignity to the conscious attempt to create literary works in an allegorical mode by explaining in his *Letter to Cangrande della Scala* that in *The Divine Comedy* he intended four levels of meaning: the literal, the allegorical (i.e., the worldly meaning), the anagogical (i.e., the other-worldly meaning) , and the tropological (i.e., the personal and moral meaning) much in accordance with the exegetical techniques used to explain certain difficult passages in the Bible. In the later Middle Ages, poets, including Chaucer in his less important works, submitted to the allegorical method as a means of defending their poems against the numerous and powerful enemies of poetry and the imagination so that always there would be a higher meaning beyond the literal meaning. This practice produced a host of major allegorical achievements ranging from *The Romance of the Rose* to the morality plays to Spenser's *Faerie Queene*. After the seventeenth-century imitators of Spenser had had their say, the allegorical method gradually fell into disfavor except for remarkable sporadic outbursts like *Pilgrim's Progress*, though allegory can be detected even in some twentieth century literary attempts.

It is ironic that the Church which dealt the deathblow to the drama was also the mother of the drama when it again reappeared in the form of tropes within the Mass itself, then with more elaborate religious dramas performed after the Mass, first within the church, then on the church steps, then in the market-place. These dramatic performances eventually developed into full-fledged cycles of miracle and mystery plays. Such a phenomenon constituted a recognition of the fact that under controlled circumstances, at least, the literary imagination could be made to serve the interests of religion.

But the pagan classics were to be heard from once again, for the Renaissance, particularly in Italy beginning about 1350, was brought about by the rediscovery of vast numbers of literary masterpieces from classical Greek and Latin writers and with it also an unbounded enthusiasm, indeed awe, for the literary greatness of these works. Writers began to imitate them and apologists began to insist more forcefully and with greater eloquence upon the value of the imagination, for it produced not only a salutary imaginative literature but also a revival of painting and sculpture and architecture and music. After Dante, literary activity was already on the increase, and under the inspiration of Dante it spread to other vernacular languages.

Boccaccio and Petrarch did much to restore classical learning in general and the prestige of the imagination in particular, not only by collecting manuscripts as they were rediscovered but by writing imaginative works in Italian as Dante had done. Other writers too began to imitate the excellence of classical literature by writing not only in Italian, but French, Spanish, and English. The lyric tradition, which Dante did much to restore, by way of the Provençal poets, was helped along by Petrarch, and a host of other lyric poets, particularly sonneteers in Italy, France, and England. The rise to prominence of lyric poetry in fact marked a major step in the restoration of the literary imagination, particularly since it owed very little to the classical tradition.

The rediscovery of Aristotle's *Poetics* also did much to give literary criticism a boost. Critics like Castelvetro, Minturno, and Scaliger saw what a remarkable document *The Poetics* was and wrote valuable and influential commentaries on it. The drama, which as I have indicated owed its rebirth to an expansion of the Catholic liturgy, and eventually evolved into the mystery and morality plays, became increasingly secular, until a full-fledged dramatic tradition was established not only in Italy but in Spain, France, and above all, England.

The phenomenon of Christian Humanism which came out of the Renaissance, did much to sanction the return of the imagination to intellectual respectability. The Christian Humanists held that not only philosophy (which St. Thomas Aquinas had helped restore) but the literary arts and history were actually not enemies but indeed the handmaidens of religion because they could promote virtuous action, which was the chief aim of religion; for virtuous action led to salvation, which in turn was, in the Church's view, the final aim of man.

The Christian Humanist movement began in Italy but in time spread to France, to Germany, and especially to England, where it particularly flourished because Christianity and Humanism were more strongly wed than in other countries. As a result, some of the greatest defenders of literature came from England, particularly in the sixteenth century. Roger Ascham, tutor to Elizabeth I and one of the most learned men in Renaissance England, recognized the moral power of literature and perceived it as a means to bring the student "first to wisdom and then to worthiness, " i.e., virtue. John Harrington in his *Brief Apology for Poetry* reflects the Christian Humanist attitude in observing that literature "ought not to be despised by the wiser sort, but to be studied and employed as was intended by the first writers and devisers thereof, which is to soften and polish the hard and rough disposition of men and make them capable of virtue and good discipline." Samuel Daniel, too, in his *Musophilus* reflects the common Christian Humanist view that poetry can lead sinful men to virtue and that it can "draw, divert, dispose, and fashion men/Better than force or rigor can direct." Spenser conceived *The Fairie Queene* as an instrument to fashion a gentleman or noble person in virtuous and gentle discipline. And Milton in the seventeenth century was happy to point out that Spenser himself is "a better teacher than Scotus or Aquinas." But it was Sir Philip Sidney's *Defense of Poesy* which may be said to represent the best statement in defense of literature of any of the Christian humanists of the Renaissance, and it remains even today one of the best cases that has ever been made for literature. His argument therefore deserves some attention here.

Sidney may be said to have built his case for literature upon the following syllogism :

Major Premise: The end of all learning is virtuous action.
Minor Premise: Of all forms of earthly learning, poetry best leads to virtuous action.
Conclusion: Therefore, poetry is the highest form of earthly learning.

In effect what he sets out to do is to demonstrate the truth of the minor premise because in the sixteenth century few disputed the truth of the major premise, so that by proving the truth of the minor premise the conclusion is inevitable.

He eliminates astronomy, the sciences, and "supernatural philosophy," i.e., astrology, alchemy, and the other "supernatural" forms of learning as major contenders on the grounds that they cannot, by their very nature, appeal to the moral sense. The astronomer, he observes, "looking to the stars might fall in a ditch"; the "inquiring philosopher [i.e., the scientist] might be blind in himself"; and the mathematician "might draw forth a straight line with a crooked heart." Thus, he concludes, "these are but serving sciences."

His argument thus leads him to take on the chief challengers to poetry as a moral force on the human personality, namely, philosophy and history. But, he observes, history deals only with the particular, and philosophy only with the general, whereas poetry deals with both, and therefore affords a higher kind of truth. "The philosopher," he concludes, "and the historian are they which would win the goal, the one by precept, the other by example. But both not having both do both halt."

Furthermore, he argues, philosophy and history merely teach because their appeal is only to the rational faculty, whereas poetry "moves," i.e., it arouses the emotions and hence reaches the will, and it is reaching the will that "moves" a person to virtue. Hence his grand conclusion: "And that moving is of a higher degree than teaching, it may by this appear, that it is well-nigh the cause and the effect of teaching. For who will be taught, if he be not moved with desire to be taught, and what so much good doth the teaching bring forth (I speak still of moral doctrine) as that it moveth one to do that which it doth teach ?"

In such fashion Sidney demonstrates the superiority of the imagination over the other human faculties as the most powerful way of leading to virtue. It is a compelling argument—as powerful today as it was at any time before, provided that the assumption still obtains that virtuous action is held in as high regard as the Christian Humanists and Christians in general regarded it. It is an argument which in turn proceeds upon the assumption that salvation is the end of life, which is the most fundamental Christian premise. Needless to say, the problem with Sidney's argument for many in the twentieth century is accepting the components of the major premise.

During the Renaissance, however, the advocates of poetry, including those whose key observations on the importance of poetry and the imagination are recorded in the Appendix of this study, were still very much on the defensive because the enemies of the imagination and the literary arts which the imagination produced were still powerful and vocal. Sidney himself with relative ease meets the most common of these arguments by countering the charges that the poet is a liar, that he corrupts the morals of his audience, that Plato expelled poets from his commonwealth, and that poetry is an idle activity.

Many of the defenses of poetry and the imagination which came out of the Renaissance, both in England and on the continent, were the result of repeated attacks upon imaginative literature that came not only from the early Christian centuries but throughout the Middle Ages, attacks which drew mainly from those in early Christianity. Plays, because of the very social nature of theatrical activity, were under attack from the time of Tertullian to the onslaughts against the stage led by Stephen Gosson and William Prynne in Puritan England. But poetry in general, particularly poetry with no exalted allegorical intentions, was still widely suspected as a threat to religion and morality even on into the seventeenth century.

Attacks upon the stage in England were renewed after the Restoration because of their questionable morality and their general disrespect for religion and the clergy. Jeremy Collier made an issue of these matters by publishing in 1698 *A Short View of the Immorality and Profaneness of the English Stage,* which set off a controversy that lasted for more than a quarter of a century. There were indeed desultory attempts to answer Collier's forceful if not always persuasive arguments, answers by Dryden and Congreve, and others who were the victims of Collier's wrath. But Collier was also answered by John Dennis, who was one of the most learned men in England and who in the whole history of literary criticism may be said to be the boldest and most assiduous champion not only of the drama but of poetry generally (since at that time there was no imaginative prose with high artistic intentions).

No sooner had Collier published his *Short View* than Dennis responded with an ambitious defense entitled *The Usefulness of the Stage* (1698) in which he endeavored no less than "to show that the stage in general is useful to the happiness of mankind, to the welfare of government, and the advancement of religion." Tragedy, he claimed, must of necessity make men virtuous: first because it moderates the passions, whose excesses cause their vices; secondly, because it instructs them in their duties both by its fable, and by the sentences." And again: "Thus, while I am pleading in defense of the stage, I am defending and supporting poetry, the best and noblest kind of writing. For all other writers are made by precept, and formed by art; but a poet prevails by the force of nature; is excited by all that is powerful in humanity, and is, sometimes, by a spirit not his own, exalted to divinity." "The Christian religion," he declares, "contains the best, nay, the only means to bring men to eternal happiness, so for the making men happy even in this life it surpasses all philosophy; but yet I confidently assert that if the stage were arrived to that degree of excellence to which in the space of some little time it may easily be brought, the frequenting of theaters would advance religion, and, consequently, the happiness of mankind, and so become a part of the Christian duty."

In another and even more ambitious treatise Dennis undertook the entire reformation of poetry by laying down the rules which would reform it and hence not only restore it but make it a powerful moral and religious force. This he did in *The Grounds for Criticism in Poetry* (1704), in the introduction to which he declared that his aim was

> to raise [poetry] to a height which it has never known before among us, and so restore it...to all its greatness and to all its innocence.

Thus, it may well be that the Western World produced no greater champion of the literary arts than John Dennis; his enthusiasm for the literary arts and his dedication to them are boundless, and perhaps no one ever made greater claims for them. In some sense it may be that if Dennis had had his way, the faculty of the imagination and hence literature would have reached its pinnacle in the early eighteenth century.

Another wise and influential voice in defense of the literary arts was to be heard before the eighteenth century was out, a voice in the old tradition, or rather the Neo-classical tradition, which above all insisted upon the moral purpose of art in general and literature in particular, namely that of Samuel Johnson. Johnson was dedicated heart and soul to the belief that imaginative literature could and did have a profound moral effect upon its audience. He reiterated Horace's famous dictum that "the aim of learning is to instruct; the aim of poetry is to instruct by pleasing." He is, one may say, the last of the great Christian Humanists, convinced as he was that philosophy and history and poetry—the three representatives of the three human faculties peculiar to man, namely reason, memory, and the imagination—could all be harnessed to make better Christians, and his pronouncements on literature, whether in his essays or in his *Lives of the Poets*, fairly breathe his fundamental conviction of the moral purpose of literature.

But in taking this stance, Johnson was already something of an anachronism. As intellectuals became less Christian, they insisted less vehemently upon the claim that poetry would make better Christians.

But even though this most powerful argument in favor of the literary arts began to lose some of its steam, the prestige of the imagination as a way of arriving at the truth about the human condition was still on the rise throughout the eighteenth century and into the nineteenth century. It is necessary to return however, for a moment, to the seventeenth century in order to identify other forces which helped to exalt the powers of the imagination.

Ironically, it was helped along in the late seventeenth century by the increasing popularity of the scientific method. The discoveries of Copernicus, Gilbert, Galileo, Harvey, Boyle, and Newton, together with the propagation of Francis Bacon's scientific vision and the founding of the Royal Society provided an enormous boost for the scientific spirit, and before the 17th century was out it had already made its mark on literature. Its first effect was that it helped dramatists and poets in England—though less so in France—to break away from the suffocating influence of strict adherence to the literary rules of Neo-classicism. Critics like Thomas Rymer and Jeremy Collier had insisted upon them, and they were the chief source of their discontent with certain literary works which they viciously attacked, Rymer the Elizabethan drama and Collier the Restoration drama. Collier in fact borrowed much from Rymer, not only his style, but his insistence upon following the classical "rules" of literature, which he used as a club to beat the naughty plays of the Restoration dramatists.

But Dryden, who was a member of the Royal Society, had developed enough independence of literary thought to part company with the French Neo-classicists and the slavish adherents to classical authority in England, and so developed a more pragmatic tack in both his criticism and his plays. So too did Sir Richard Blackmore, whose poetry did not do him much credit, but whose *Essay upon Epic Poetry* (1716) repudiated the authority of Aristotle's *Poetics*, just as Bacon and the Royal Society had repudiated most of the rest of Aristotle. And being a physician himself and a fellow of the College of Physicians, Blackmore absorbed the scientific spirit so thoroughly that he was delighted to see the authority of Aristotle overthrown by leading intellectuals and wondered that his authority in matters of literature had not likewise been overthrown: "It is wonderful that the effect was not more extensive," he wrote. "They had as great reason to have proceeded to the examination of the art of poetry, and to have made enquiry into those who settled on better foundations."

This new assertion of artistic independence was abetted by the literary views of Edward Young, who in his essay entitled *Conjectures on Original Composition* (1759) recommended, as his title suggests, a new emphasis upon inspired genius and creative imagination as opposed to slavish imitation of ancient writers, which the rigid Neo-classicists had insisted upon as the only hope for literature in the vernacular. Just as Bacon and the members of The Royal Society had insisted upon the liberty to investigate and experiment with nature, so Young insisted upon the same freedom for poets. Young was a latter-day participant in the controversy between the ancients and the moderns; and he clearly comes out on the side of the moderns. In fact, he insists that the only way the English can produce a great literature is to go their own way and to stop going the way of the ancient writers. "Let it not be suspected," he wrote, "that I would weakly insinuate anything in favor of the moderns as compared with the ancient authors; no, I am lamenting their great inferiority. But I think it is no necessary inferiority; that it is not from divine destination, but from a cause far beneath the moon; I think that human souls, through all periods are equal, that due care and exertion would set us nearer our predecessors than we are at present."

Young's essay is permeated with the spirit of Bacon, particularly Bacon's insistence upon overturning authority in favor of experimentation, and in fact Young acknowledged his debt to Bacon in his own insistence upon the independence of poets from classical authority.

The authors of imaginative literature during the earlier eighteenth century were so far from being fearful of any threat of science that satirists like Pope and Swift did not hesitate to ridicule the new preoccupation with science. But the scientific spirit under the aegis of the Royal Society did fire a shot across the bow of *belles lettres* by recommending that English prose be liberated from the unscientific use of language, particularly rhetoric and metaphor and figures of speech generally, in the interests of a greater accuracy. Francis Bacon had himself warned against the abuse of language in *The Advancement of Learning* and made a great point of deploring the writing of those who put manner before matter; indeed he regarded such abuse as a major hindrance to the advancement of learning. The Royal Society, under the banner of Bacon, launched a major crusade to urge its members to be less emotional and more factual in the use of language. Thomas

Spratt in his *History of the Royal Society* (1667) speaks of the members' resolution "to reject all the amplifications, digressions, and swellings of style" and "to return back to the primitive purity, and shortness, when men delivered as many *things*, almost in an equal number of *words*." And there was indeed evidence that this scientific crusade against rhetoric had its effect upon major members of the Society, including Joseph Glanville, Abraham Cowley, John Tillotson, and even Dryden himself, who admitted that whatever talent he showed for English prose he owed to the work of Bishop Tillotson. These developments represent early examples of the scientific pre-occupation with language which was to consume linguistic and analytical philosophers in the 20th century and much modern literary criticism as well. An even more ominous threat to the literary arts and indeed to the authority of language in general came from Thomas Hobbes, who claimed that words are only the marks of things, and who in a somewhat primitive way called into question the whole problem of the use of words to represent reality. To some degree he foreshadows the deconstructionist position, which will be discussed in the second chapter.

But these rumbling threats of science against the literary arts remained rumblings for some two and a half centuries. Meanwhile, the prestige of the imagination gathered steam in good part being fueled by the spirit of science, which emboldened writers to renounce their dependence upon classical models and to look into their hearts and write. Edward Young in his *Conjectures on Original Composition* was also riding on a new intellectual development which further strengthened the prestige of the imagination, namely the idea of the natural goodness of man. This idea of man as having escaped Adam and Eve's curse of Original Sin was reborn in England, spread, if somewhat unenthusiastically, at least at first, to France, and hit with full force a newly aroused German intellectual tradition in the eighteenth century.

The idea of the natural goodness of man was in part a reaction to the Calvinistic doctrine of total depravity, which insisted that Christ would redeem only selective inveterate sinners, and partly to Thomas Hobbes, who insisted upon the total selfishness of all human motives but who denied the possibility of any promise of salvation on the grounds that there is no God and therefore no Redeemer. Since these views were not well calculated to gain adherents, and were in fact generally abhorrent, the inclination was to take the opposite position, namely that natural man is naturally good, and that his instincts, his emotions, and perhaps even his whims could be trusted.

The net effect of the increasing rise of the popularity among intellectuals in the eighteenth century of the idea of the natural goodness of man was to contribute to the destruction of the authority of Christianity, because virtually all of the key doctrines of Christianity depend upon the doctrine of the Fall. But religion's loss was literature's gain, because the idea of the natural goodness of man also meant the idea of the natural goodness of the poet, including his emotions, which, as Edward Young seemed to suggest, could now be expressed with greater freedom, with greater certainty and confidence, and indeed with greater inspiration, and hence greater authority and truth.

Thus the prestige of literature was to rise higher in the early nineteenth century under the aegis of the Romantics even than it had in the eighteenth century, under the aegis of the Enlighteners and the Neo-classicists, who still insisted that the poet is fallible and that the errors and weaknesses in his work must still be carefully identified by the watchdogs of literary criticism.

As a result of the declining role of religion in the search for truth, and, among the romantics, the declining role of mere reason (i.e. philosophy), the imagination renewed its claim as the best method of guiding mankind to where it ought to be going. Shelley was certain that poets are "the unacknowledged legislators of the world," and Matthew Arnold went so far as to insist that poetry, above all other forms of learning whatsoever—including religion—would become the highest source of truth. In a famous passage he predicts that "more and more mankind will discover that we have to turn to poetry to interpret life for us, to console us, and to sustain us. Without poetry, our science will appear incomplete; and most of what now passes for religion and philosophy will be replaced by poetry." In a sense the claims which Matthew Arnold made for poetry are greater than those of either Sir Philip Sidney or John Dennis, for Sidney and Dennis still regarded poetry as the handmaiden of religion, not a substitute for it, and thus represented a continuation of the Christian Humanist tradition. Arnold, on the other hand, insisted that there is no higher form of learning than poetry, because having lost his faith along with most of the other highly influential nineteenth century intellectuals, he could not admit the superiority of religion and the Scriptures.

Thus, poetry in the eyes of a substantial number of nineteenth century intellectuals was indeed the queen of the sciences. But its reign was not to be for long, because the insistent voices of science and the scientific spirit were becoming not only more persuasive but more aggressive. It was not the imagination, the science-oriented intellectuals insisted, that would lead most certainly to truth, but the senses; and the achievements of science had more and more evidence to support their claims. From the Copernican theory of the universe to the Darwinian theory of evolution, the scientific method had amassed a series of material victories so impressive that it seemed as though the senses had overwhelmed the imagination in the search for truth. Imaginative literature, after all, created only an imaginative world; the truth of it could not be measured by scientific methods, and its relation to reality was therefore suspect if not nil.

Indeed the defenders of imaginative literature in the early nineteenth century were not so complacent about the threat of the scientific method to their own method as Pope and Swift had been. Virtually all of the Romantic poets, for example, were aware of the encroachments of science upon the world of the imagination, and poets like Wordsworth, Coleridge, and Shelley, all expressed their disdain for the growing supremacy of the scientific method. William Blake in particular, because of his unorthodox visionary bent, fulminated against it.

Thomas De Quincey's defense of imaginative literature echoes that of Sir Philip Sidney even in language in his well-known distinction between "literature of knowledge and literature of power" (i.e., imaginative literature). Literature of power, he observed, engages the emotions and hence works a more powerful effect upon the mind than mere expository prose. Hence, he concluded, "the preeminency [of the imaginative writer] over all other authors who merely *teach*, of the meanest that moves, or that teaches if at all, indirectly by moving."

Thomas Carlyle too had exalted the role of the poet in society by making him one of his heroes. "The true poet is ever, as of old," he declared, "the Seer; whose eye has been gifted to discern the godlike Mystery of God's Universe and decipher some new lines of its celestial writing; we can still call him a *Vates*, and Seer; for he *sees* into the greatness of secrets, 'the open secret'; hidden things become clear; how the future...is but another phase of the Present; thereby are his words in very truth prophetic; what he has spoken shall be done."

*****

But there were early warnings that literature was in the process of losing its authority. As far back as the later seventeenth century Thomas Spratt had observed that "when the fabulous Age was past, philosophy took a little more Courage; and ventured to rely upon its own strength, without the assistance of poetry." By the middle of the nineteenth century not only philosophy but science took "a little more courage" and even went so far in some quarters as to attack the pretenses of imaginative literature.

Thomas Love Peacock, himself a satirical novelist, ventured a prophecy in 1820. The poet, he observed, " lives in the days that are past. In whatever degree poetry is cultivated, it must necessarily be to the neglect of some branch of useful study"; and he draws for the reader a picture in which the mathematicians, astronomers, chemists, and even the historians, politicians, and political economists from their great intellectual heights look down upon a "modern Parnassus far beneath them and knowing how small a place it occupies in the comprehensiveness of their prospect, smile at the little ambition and the circumscribed perceptions with which the drivelers and mountbanks upon it are contending for the poetical palm and the critical chair."

Macaulay had his own dim view of the future of poetry in face of the new scientific threat to it. "In an enlightened age," he predicted," there will be much intelligence, much science, much philosophy, abundance of just classification and subtle analysis, abundance of wit and eloquence, but little poetry....As the magic lantern acts best in a dark room, poetry effects its purpose most completely in a dark age." By 1882, Thomas Henry Huxley, one of the great interpreters of Darwin, felt able to write that "For the purposes of attaining real culture, an exclusively scientific education is at least as efficacious as an exclusively literary education."

It is not necessary here to even attempt to describe how widely and how heavily the influence of science and the scientific method spread through the intellectual life of nineteenth century Europe. It created the Higher Criticism, which, by applying the scientific method to the Scriptures, destroyed the authority of the Bible, and hence dealt a crippling blow to religion; it heavily influenced economic thought and political thought; and it created the social sciences, especially sociology and psychology as disciplines by applying the scientific method of counting and measuring in order to attempt to arrive at laws of human behavior. History too became increasingly scientized as more emphasis was placed upon piling fact upon fact as historians grew less willing to make moral judgments of historical events or historical figures. The same thing, logically, developed in the genre of biography inasmuch as biographers began to search for every conceivable detail about the life of the subject and far less likely than say Plutarch or Samuel Johnson to make judgmental observations about them. The art of pedagogy was reduced to a science. All this in addition to continued spectacular discoveries in biology, physics, chemistry, and geology resulted in the scientizing of virtually every field of human knowledge.

Auguste Comte, the French sociologist, summed up the advent of the scientific method as the surest approach to truth in his little treatise entitled *The Three Stages of Civilization*, in which he identified the primitive stage of civilization as the Age of Faith, which lasted from the earliest times until the latter part of the seventeenth century; the intermediate stage: the Age of Reason, from the middle of the seventeenth century until the middle of the nineteenth century; and the third and final stage, the Age of Science, the beginnings of which he himself was trimphantly announcing. Poetry came to be associated with the primitive stage, as Spratt and Macaulay had foretold.

After the great claims which Matthew Arnold had made for imaginative literature, even as late as 1880, it has been all down hill for the faculty of the imagination, which in a more practical, indeed pragmatic age, began more and more to lose out to what Peacock had called the "useful" branches of knowledge. The Utilitarian movement in England was not much help either. By the lights of Jeremy Bentham, imaginative literature had no consequential role to play in the future society, though John Stuart Mill tried mightily to consider the advantages of poetry to society, and with some success. But the ages of the eloquent arguments of Aristotle, Sidney, Dennis, Johnson, and Arnold, and a whole host of other dauntless defenders of the literary imagination were, it seemed, ended even before the arrival of the twentieth century.

It is not to be supposed, therefore, that literary theory and criticism or indeed literature itself and the perception of the value of literature would be any less affected than any of the other branches of learning. How badly imaginative literature and the literary imagination have fared in the twentieth century, particularly in America, and particularly as they fell victim to science, technology, and the scientific spirit, is the subject of the next three chapters.

Chapter II

Modern Critical Theory and the Trivializing of Literature

This chapter takes up the sensitive task of demonstrating how literary theory and literary criticism for more than a century have been gradually trivializing literature to the point that it has lost virtually all the prestige and authority it enjoyed under the aegis of the great literary critics from Aristotle to Matthew Arnold. Almost no one any longer believes that literature is the highest form of learning, or even a major form of learning. In some highly placed circles, even in colleges and universities, it has often come to be little more than an optional field of study, not much more worthy perhaps than dozens of other fields. Wherever it is still highly regarded it is in spite of contemporary literary theorists rather than on account of them.

How did this plunge in the prestige of the literary arts come about? The best answer seems to be that some two centuries ago highly influential literary theorists began to latch on to certain philosophical principles—particularly regarding the nature of man, the nature of literature, and the nature of language—which have now done much to destroy its prestige as a major cultural force, particularly in America. Four stages can perhaps be identified to describe the gradual decline of the role of literature as a major cultural force. The first stage separated literature from morality; the second stage separated literature from the audience; the third separated literature from reality; and the fourth, though it sought to restore the importance of literature to the audience and to reality, has politicized literature and so has demeaned it in a different way. I should like to make some observations on each of them.

The first stage, which separates literature from morality, took two forms: first literature as self-expression in the romantic tradition, and second, literature as art-for-art's sake in the hedonistic tradition. This stage began to develop in the late eighteenth century and ran through the nineteenth and, in both forms, well into the twentieth century.

As the last chapter pointed out, for the early Greeks and again for Renaissance intellectuals the literary arts held an exalted place in the hierarchy of learning. The defenders of poetry during the Renaissance could in fact make even higher claims for the moral purpose of literature than could the Greeks, for they insisted that its potentially profound moral influence could do something to promote salvation, which was, and still is, to some extent, the aim of life in the Christian view. It was a claim that the Greeks could not make. The moral force of literature was basically the argument of Sidney in his *Defense of Poetry,* and it was the argument too of John Dennis and Samuel Johnson, among others. A glimpse of how highly literature was esteemed during the Renaissance and well into the eighteenth century because of its moral effect upon the audience can be had by scanning the "Literary Declarations" in the Appendix to this study.

*****

As a direct result of this Christian orientation, the later seventeenth century may be thought of as the age of "judicial criticism," because the term emphasizes that the duty of the critic above all is to judge a literary work on the basis of a set of generally accepted criteria which were both moral and aesthetic. These included the Neo-classical canon of "rules," which were derived in part from Horace and elaborated upon by Italian Renaissance critics and then by French and English Neo-classical critics. Without describing the details of these "rules," I wish merely to point out the fact that there appeared in England, but also in France, a school of criticism which was criticism in the best sense. It insisted that the critic's task is to *judge* the moral and aesthetic value of a literary work. Its representatives were professional evaluators and judgers, not merely appreciators or explicators. They were exactly, as we shall see, what most modern and contemporary critics are not.

Since virtually all of these critics stressed the moral purpose of art against a background of Christian morality, they found a ready criterion for determining which works were good and which were bad. Nor was morality the sole concern in their analyses of literary works. Even Jeremy Collier, who built a career by attacking the immorality of the stage, made forays into the aesthetic aspects of the drama, and much of this practical criticism included such influential critics as Thomas Rymer, John Dryden, John Dennis, and Joseph Addison. Their criticism was based upon the fundamental premise that man's moral nature is flawed, that it therefore needs to be reformed, and that literature is a powerful means of reforming it. That assessment of man's moral nature had been shared by the most influential philosophers and intellectuals from Ancient Greece through the Renaissance and on into the eighteenth century. This kind of criticism became known as the "beauties-and-faults" school of criticism, in which the critic considered that his chief duty was to call attention to both the beauties and the faults of a literary work.

The finest hour of the judicial school of criticism came probably with the literary criticism of Samuel Johnson, who was easily the most compelling member of the group because of his literary style, the force of his generalizations, and his literary intelligence. His *Preface to Shakespeare* and the third sections of his major *Lives of the Poets* represent the highest point in the tradition of judicial criticism. Johnson believed as much in the moral powers of literature as any other critic, and he brought his critical genius to bear on many of the best poets in England. But Johnson's judicial criticism marks the end of an era; in fact his kind of criticism was already becoming an anachronism. It was gradually being replaced by what I have called "good-natured criticism."

As might be suspected, the rise of good-natured criticism as a replacement for judicial criticism was a complex process, and the transition began subtly and indeed unintentionally. It began with the increasingly influential idea of the natural goodness of man, which, as the last chapter indicated, had the effect initially of exalting the role of the imagination and hence of the literary arts as a source of truth. But this new emphasis upon man's natural goodness led inevitably to the idea of the natural goodness of poets, including their emotions, so the idea became to express these inspired emotions. There was thus a new emphasis upon originality, genius, inspiration, and self-expression.

If man's emotional nature is itself good and trustworthy, as much romantic writing was to assume, then, as Walter Jackson Bate, an historian of literary criticism, observed," the ideal course [for the poet] to follow is to express his feelings—to regard less traditions and customs and look into his heart and write." The poet's uniqueness and the originality of his genius became more important than the representation of universality in human nature, such as most literary theorists had insisted upon from the time of Aristotle.

From the middle of the eighteenth century onward, as this new view of man became increasingly popular, literary critics began to talk more and more about the poet expressing his emotions than the effect his work had upon the audience. The net result of this development was that the poet felt less and less responsible for communicating to the reader his inspired emotions and the motive for his emotions and more and more concerned simply with getting them expressed. As Irving Babbitt observed, the effect on the poet is something like the relief or sense of achievement that a hen gets from laying an egg. The eventual net result of the idea of literature as self-expression was to abandon all responsibility to its audience and hence to abandon the longstanding duty of the poet to produce a beneficial moral effect upon the audience through the practice of his art. If man was, in effect, immaculately conceived—if he was *naturally* good—then his instincts and emotions must also be naturally good. Plato and the whole traditional view of man's nature must be wrong; so too the traditional view of the final cause of literature; and indeed the whole traditional understanding of the creative process must be wrong. Controlling the emotions in art or trying to understand them became less important than expressing them. Free expression of the emotions was supposed to lead to liberation and truth and ecstasy. The poetic effusions of the nineteenth century poets became free-verse secretions in the twentieth. The long-term result, which I will discuss more at length in the final chapter of this study, was to lead poetry down the path of obscurantism, formlessness, unintelligibility, and sometimes even fraudulence.

The good-natured school of criticism which grew out of this development gathered steam during the nineteenth century and is still widespread in the twentieth century. Negative judgments of literary works became more and more confined to journalistic writers and book reviewers, as professional literary critics spent their efforts admiring the works that they liked and ignoring the bad works which they no longer had a right to dislike. The faults of a literary work became untouchable, or at least untouched. Even Matthew Arnold had lost the sense of the critic's duty to protect society from bad literature as he concentrated on propagating "the best that has been thought and said in the world" to the neglect of the worst that has been thought and said in the world, even when it sometimes passed for the best.

A little book by Helen Gardner entitled *The Business of Criticism* (1966) captures the spirit of the modern good-natured critic. "The rudiments of criticism," she observed, " is not so much the power to distinguish any good poem from any bad poem, as the power to respond to a good poem and to be able to elucidate its significance, beauty, and meaning in terms which are valid for other readers." Gardner explicitly repudiates the idea that literary critics "should keep a strict eye over the Miscarriages of our Authors," as Thomas Rymer put it, or that they should "detect and disgrace Errour," as John Dennis put it. "Critics," she says, "are wise to leave alone those works which they feel a call to deflate." She refers to an allegory by Samuel Johnson in which Literary Criticism bears the Scepter, which was given her by Justice, and the Torch, which was manufactured by Labor and lighted by Truth. Applying this allegory to herself, Gardner states flatly, *"I do not feel any call to wield the scepter."* (Italics are Gardner's). Not many critics, either in the nineteenth or the twentieth century, are that blunt about avoiding the responsibilities which Rymer and Dennis and Johnson regarded as crucial to the critic's calling, but the spirit of good-natured criticism remains, and the spirit of judicial criticism has virtually disappeared except in book reviews and journalists' columns.

In effect, what good-natured critics did was to separate literature from morality by refusing to judge a literary work on moral grounds, in good part because they more and more thought of literature as self-expression, in accordance with the increasingly popular idea of the natural goodness of man and hence the natural goodness of the poet's emotions. Critics thought of their chief duty as interpreting and appreciating the author's works rather than judging them, and hence in effect repudiated the fundamental premise of the purpose of literature which Neo-classical critics considered crucial to the dignity and esteem in which literature should be held.

*****

The rise of another theory, however, which also contributed to the separation of literature from morality, was the idea of literature for literature's sake, or more commonly described as art-for-art's sake.

This was a much more self-conscious movement. Its early advocates made a loud point of declaring the independence of literature from morality, and in doing so, made another major contribution to the trivializing of literature. For if the end of literature is unalloyed pleasure without the burden of being moral, then it must be concluded that, since there are pleasures and pleasures, one may be justified in preferring the pleasure of a glass of fine whiskey to the pleasure of a fine poem or novel. And among absolute relativists, who is to say which is more pleasurable and therefore preferable?

*****

The formation of the art-for-art's sake school began with the German Romantic critics, who invented aesthetics as a means of detaching literature from morality. Its origins lay in Immanuel Kant's idea that beautiful objects have no specific purpose. The movement in literature may be said to have been historically highlighted by the thinking of Schelling and Schiller in Germany, continued by Coleridge and Pater in England, by Baudelaire and the French Symbolists in France, and by Edgar Allan Poe in America. It continued, as we shall see, in much critical theory in America at least up through the 1950s. In effect these critics took the position that literature does not and should not take its value, its importance, its reason for being, from its moral effect upon the audience, but solely from its pleasurable effect. It was a position which, like the theory of literature as self-expression, repudiated a critical tradition reaching all the way back to the ancient Greeks and continuing well into the nineteenth century.

Edgar Allan Poe was one of the most obvious advocates of art-for-art's sake in America. In *The Poetic Principle*, for example, he observes:

> We have taken it into our heads that to write a poem simply for the poem's sake and to acknowledge such to have been our design, would be to confess ourselves radically wanting in the true poetic dignity and force:—but the simple fact is, that, would we but permit ourselves to look into our souls we should immediately there discover that under the sun there neither exists not can exist any work more thoroughly dignified—this poem, which is a poem and nothing more—this poem written solely for the poem's sake.

It should perhaps be pointed out here that the phrase art-for-art's-sake is a misnomer in that it does not make sense to say that the poem is written for the poem's sake. The poem has no sake; it doesn't care about itself. Poetry must be written for the sake of *somebody*, either an audience or the poet himself or herself. As it turns out, what Poe meant is the unadulterated pleasure of the reader of the poem, delight without any moral strings attached. Thus Poe is an early and distinguished alumnus of the so-called art-for-art's sake school. He maintained not only that the object of poetry is mere beauty but that indeed the subject is mere beauty. He acknowledged that "the incitements of passion or the precepts of duty or even the lessons of Truth may...be introduced into a poem, and with advantage; for they may subserve incidentally, by various ways, the general purpose of the poem." But Poe's use of the word "may" and "subserve" and above all "incidentally" make it clear that "passion" and the "precepts of duty" and even, as he says, "the lessons of truth" are *not* the essential ingredients of any good poem. Hence his conclusion that the poem should be "written solely for the poem's sake." Lacking as he did any understanding of how a literary work can be moral without having a moral, and having properly rejected what he called the "didactic heresy," he was pretty well forced to conclude that literature is "just for fun," as they say, albeit great fun, and that the essence of its value lies purely in the pleasure and beauty it can provide. He would not even agree to Keats's equation of Truth and Beauty.

The great French poet Baudelaire became intrigued with Poe's attempt to strip literature of its moral value, and he too concluded that art has no relation to morality. Poetry, said Baudelaire, "has no other end but itself. Beauty, not truth is its object." Having rejected the didactic heresy he adopted with Poe the hedonistic heresy. In part due to Baudelaire's fascination with Poe, the entire Symbolist movement in poetry did much to bring about the final, if theoretical break between literature and morality. Meanwhile, Walter Pater, the philosopher *par excellence* of pure hedonism was participating in the destruction of the dignity of literature even while he thought he was elevating it. He is well known for his statement in the Conclusion to *The Renaissance* that "to burn always with that hard gemlike flame is success in life," as well as his declaration that "art comes to you professing frankly to give nothing but the highest quality to your moments as they pass, and simply for those moments' sake." It is true that when Pater discovered that he had inadvertently become a spokesman for a hedonistic view of life as a result of his famous remarks, he qualified his position later in *Marius the Epicurean.*

But it should be recognized that the *fin-de-siècle* art-for-art's sake phenomenon was only a part of the steady movement in the late nineteenth century and the earlier twentieth century toward a purely hedonistic aesthetic which could boast the support of such influential thinkers as Benedetto Croce in Italy, Henri Bergson in France, and George Santayana in America, among others. Hedonism in art, it would seem, was here to stay, at least at the theoretical level. "We have done with the moral judgment of literature," said Joel Spingarn in his 1910 lecture on "The New Criticism"; and although literary theorists were not quite done with it then, they are in most circles done with it now.

*****

The second stage in the history of literary criticism which led to the trivializing of literature began with the rising influence of science upon letters in the nineteenth century. In the previous chapter I pointed out that major developments in the intellectual history of the West, particularly during the course of the past 150 years, undermined the prestige of literature by advancing the method of science over the method of the imagination as the best way to arrive at truth. The influence of science has been so telling that there can be no doubt that it is in good part responsible for the waning influence of literature upon society, particularly in America.

But it was not the duty of the intellectuals who brought about this revolution either to save or to promote the literary arts. They simply followed their own lights in determining how best to arrive at truth, and they concluded that the scientific method was the way. In the process, the works of the imagination, including the literary arts, lost much of their authority and prestige. But the point I wish to emphasize here is that the literary theorists aided and abetted the fall of the prestige of literature by submitting themselves to the very scientific spirit which was undermining the discipline which they represented. In effect, they "scientized" literature, and hence collaborated with those intellectuals who insisted that the method of the sciences is superior to the method of the imagination as a source of truth.

The fashioning of a literary theory under the influence of the scientific method may be said to have begun with two highly influential French critics: Charles-Augustin Sainte-Beuve and Hippolyte Taine. Sainte-Beuve's critical position owes a great deal to the romantic notion of the poet as original genius and to the idea of art as self-expression, but it owes even more to the rising scientific spirit. Sainte-Beuve become so obsessed with the idea that a literary work is essentially an expression of the author's soul that he insisted that a scrupulous knowledge of the author is crucial to a true understanding of his work. "Unless one has faced a certain number of questions about an author," he observed, "and until one has answered them, one cannot be sure of capturing him completely, even though these questions seem completely unrelated to the character of his writings. What did he think religiously? How was he affected by the sight of nature. How did he act so far as women are concerned?—or in the matter of money? Was he rich—was he poor?—None of the answers to these questions is unimportant in judging the author of a book—and the book itself, if the work is not a treatise on pure geometry; especially if it is a literary work, a work into which he enters at all." Sainte-Beuve still held on to the idea that literature ought to have a moral effect upon its audience, but this new interest in the relation of the author to his work began to be pursued with such vigor that it led to a biographical approach to literature and may properly be called biographical criticism. It also led to the increasing glorification of the mere fact as an end in itself, an emphasis which became a major consequence of the effect of the scientific method upon literary studies.

One of the consequences of this new scientific scrutiny which Sainte-Beuve advocated was the production of what can best be called scientific biographies in which nothing about the writer is omitted, however seemingly trivial. The two-volume life-and-letters brand of biography in the nineteenth century gave way to the multi-volumed biographies of the twentieth century, often with sanitary objectivity. Many of them have become so voluminous that they have passed out of the realm of the biographer's art and have become merely sourcebooks.

Taine carried Sainte-Beuve's concern for the writer's life a good deal farther by including not only extensive biographical facts, but his social and historical environment, and his literary sources. Taine's *History of Literature* (1863) therefore marks a wider role for the literary critic by emphasizing every conceivable source of influence upon the writer and with a scientific thoroughness. These developments drew less and less attention to the effect of literature upon the reader, both moral and aesthetic, and more and more attention to the author, so that a further boost was given to separating the literary arts from their broad moral and aesthetic function.

This zealous concern for the literary fact, or more often the extra-literary fact, caused the tradition of good-natured criticism gradually to merge with the tradition of what may be called "denatured criticism," i.e., criticism which neither criticizes nor appreciates, but which is preoccupied exclusively with explaining and elucidating, i.e., criticism which is not criticism at all but merely scholarship under the increasing influence of the scientific spirit and the exaltation of the mere fact.

But the literary theories of Sainte-Beuve and Taine marked only the beginning of the scientizing of literary theory. Historical criticism and scholarship, in which they showed the way, exerted a tremendous influence especially in Europe, where it gave rise to the relentlessly thorough methods of German scholarship. But it also made an indelible mark on English and American scholars in their frantic search for facts, oftentimes merely for the sake of the facts, and in the belief that an endless compilation of facts would somehow point to the truth, including the truths of the human condition.

The increasing popularity of the biographical and historical approach to literature and the consequent scientizing of literary criticism was merely the beginning of the era of the denatured critic. The next stage was the arrival of the formalist critics, who, by way of reacting to what seemed to them the excessive search for extra-literary facts, insisted upon concentrating on the form of the literary work without reference to any outside influence or concern. They were themselves products of the scientific spirit in their scrupulously close reading of literary texts and their attempt to exhaust everything that was to be said about a literary work by merely examining the work itself—without relating it either to the author or to the audience.

I. A. Richards may be said to have started off the movement with his *Principles of Literary Criticism* (1925) in which he maintained a sanitized scientific approach to literature by measuring it in accordance with the neurological response of the reader and hence established a purely quantitative criterion. He rejected even the slightest suggestion of a qualitative approach, either aesthetic or moral. William Empson with his emphasis upon "ambiguity" in literature carried on Richards' spirit of avoiding evaluation.

American critics like John Crowe Ransom, Alan Tate, and Cleanth Brooks sought out with scientific zeal such phenomena as paradox, tension, and texture in literature, particularly in poetry. Thus in their way they also avoided dealing with the moral effect of literature upon the audience, and unlike Rymer and Dennis and Samuel Johnson, they did not engage in the practice of correcting taste. Theirs was hothouse criticism of the highest order.

What was happening in this development first of biographical and historical criticism and then of formalist criticism is that the critics were gradually being transformed into mere scholars. They became professional literary exegetes and explicators, and in the process they ignored entirely or almost entirely the effect of literature upon the audience. From the works of the American branch of formalists, specifically the New Critics, it is virtually impossible to find any good reason why a student should take a literature course in school or why anyone should devote a day or a life to literature. They are called formalist critics because their exclusive concern was with what Aristotle called the "formal cause" of literature, and not the "final cause." This almost total neglect of the purpose of literature necessarily had the effect of trivializing it.

Certainly they did not defend the moral purpose of literature, and there are in fact grounds for suspicion that their view of the purpose of literature was essentially hedonistic. On one occasion one of the New Critics was forced to the wall and made to show his hand on the crucial question of the purpose of literature. The occasion was a controversy between Yvor Winters and John Crowe Ransom over the question of just what literature *is* for. Ransom was so much an exponent of the New Criticism that he popularized the term and wrote a book with that title. Yvor Winters has been commonly associated with the New Critics, and indeed he employed many of the same meticulous methods of elucidating a poem or novel that had been the hallmark of the New Criticism, but the *differences* between Winters and the New Critics are far more crucial. Winters was one of the few modern critics, particularly the few American critics, who still insisted upon the moral purpose of literature, much in the tradition of Dennis and Johnson, though without their Christian orientation. In this position he stood almost alone, except for a few critics like Irving Babbitt and Paul Elmer More, who also devoted their lives to attempting to emphasize the universal social and moral value of literature, though they often did so without proper attention to aesthetic considerations.

Winters was not guilty of ignoring the aesthetic aspects of literature; in fact he insisted upon them while at the same time insisting too upon the moral effect of literary works upon the audience. Winters pointed out in his *In Defense of Reason* that all literature deals with human experience and that "it can therefore be understood only on moral terms." All writers in some sense, he insisted, unconsciously or inadvertently comment upon or judge that human experience by communicating the feelings which, ideally at least, ought to be motivated by the proper understanding of the experience. I shall not enlarge here upon Winter's theory except to say that in his insistence upon the moral purpose of literature he carefully and emphatically rejected the didactic theory, not only on the grounds that most literature is not didactic but on the grounds that literature does not have to have a moral to be moral.

But Ransom, whether in *The New Criticism* or *The World's Body*, cannot understand the distinction which Winters makes between Winters' own "moralistic" theory and the didactic theory, and as a result, like Poe, he rejects the didactic theory in favor of the only alternative he feels is open to him, namely the hedonistic theory. Ransom's discussion of the Christian humanist view of literature is palpably patronizing, and he is downright contemptuous of Winters' demonstration of the relationship between literature and morality. Winters, for his part, pointed out in his essay "Thunder Without God" that Ransom renders literature contemptible by denying its moral nature and purpose. Ransom is forced to conclude, observed Winters, that "Poetry is an obscure form of self-indulgence, a search for excitement." Many of the New Critics would perhaps be reluctant to follow Ransom into the hedonistic argument, though they have not, as I indicated, done much to argue against it either.

But, sparring over the final cause of literature is rare in the twentieth century because any discussion of the purpose of literature has become rare. The general direction of literary criticism after the *fin-de-siècle* hedonists and after the biographical and historical critics and the formalists has been relentlessly more toward scholarship, explication, and exegesis.

But the New Critics did not have everything their own way in insisting that literary works be studied to the exclusion of all outside references. Subsequent to the rise of the biographical and historical approach to literature described earlier in this chapter, critics continued to plunder literature for its extra-literary values, increasingly at the expense of both its universal moral and aesthetic values. There followed the rise of psychological criticism, sociological criticism, psychoanalytical criticism, anthropological criticism, and myth and symbolist criticism, to name some of the more prominent schools which served the special interests of scholar-critics and which therefore undervalued the power and universal appeal of the best literature. In fact, all of these approaches get farther and farther away from true criticism, and all such approaches helped to establish the function of the critic as mere scholar, whose duty did not extend beyond fact-seeking.

I do not wish to undervalue the contributions which scholarship of this kind has made to an appreciation and understanding of literature; some of them have been immense. But in the process, literary theory lost sight of the proper role of the literary critic, which is to distinguish between the better and the worse among literary works as aesthetic and moral triumphs or failures, and why. In fact, what these "theories" of literature have in common is that they are not theories of literature at all. A literary theory, in order to be a genuine theory, must deal at the outset with the most fundamental of all theoretical questions about literature, namely: What is its purpose, its *raison d'être*? As we have seen, virtually all the major literary critics from Aristotle and Horace through the Middle Ages and the Renaissance, and indeed through the eighteenth century and even most of the nineteenth century insisted as their starting point that literature does have a purpose, that it is an exalted purpose, and that that purpose is the moral and aesthetic effect upon the audience. Some modern "schools" of criticism such as I have mentioned have become so obsessed with the fact-seeking approach to literature that they do not even ask the question, and as a result they have for the most part abandoned literary criticism for mere literary scholarship. This failure to define the purpose of literature is what makes twentieth century literary criticism sterile and desiccated and which thus trivializes literature itself.

*****

We come now to the third stage of the story of the trivializing of literature in the twentieth century, namely the separation of literature from reality. While English and American critics in their innocence were trying to squeeze from literature its biographical, historical, anthropological, sociological, symbolic, and occasionally its aesthetic value, there were more sinister, more cynical, and perhaps ultimately more influential forces at work on the European continent which were to challenge, if not demolish their efforts. These forces came out of France, and their business was to scrutinize as never before the meaning of the little words which make up the great works on which all previous critics had been spending their energies. I refer to the structuralists and the post-structuralists.

Structuralism is commonly recognized as having had its beginnings in the work of the Swiss linguist Ferdinand de Saussure in the early twentieth century, though the semiotic theories of Charles E. Peirce, the nineteenth century American linguist, bore strong similarities. Saussure's intention was to put the science of language on a firm footing by declaring that language is a system of signs which can be investigated scientifically. This approach, however, required the elimination of the unscientific part of language, namely the author, who uses it in his attempt to represent reality. Only the signifier (sound image like the word "dog) and the signified (like the concept of "dog") were left. Saussure's vision was much abetted by the thinking of the anthropologist Claude Levi-Straus and the early thinking of Roland Barthes, both of whom extended the idea of language as a system of signs to include all aspects of human culture, and to extend the meaning of the word "text" to include everything which had a structure and which could be reduced to a system of signs. The structuralists went even further: they insisted that everything is a text because the mind cannot comprehend anything that is not a "text." The structuralists, however, insisted that these "texts" were logically consistent and therefore subject to scientific investigation.

Even though structuralism influenced virtually every discipline that deals with words, from anthropology to religion, its focal point was literature. Structuralists practiced their arts far more on literary "texts" than on philosophical or historical or anthropological texts, and hence their importance to the discussion here.

Such revolutionary concepts were at first plentifully opposed by many intellectuals because the exclusive emphasis upon form without consideration of the human value of the "texts" made structuralism a militant anti-humanist movement; it rejected everything that the humanities all the way back to the ancient Greek thinkers stood for. But ultimately it is not easy to ignore, because it represents one more aspect of the scientific spirit at work. After all, the scientific method had been applied to human behavior and thus produced the semi-disciplines of anthropology, sociology, psychology, and economics. It had also been applied to history, to biography, to pedagogy and even to religion. It was even applied to literature and literary criticism. Why should it not also be applied to language? And so it was. Structuralism is anti-humanistic just as every application of the scientific method to human activity must be at least non-humanistic. The scientific method also seeks facts, not values; it is by definition incapable of dealing with values. It cannot tell us anything about the eternal and crucial ethical problems of "ought."

Even though structuralism was of European origin, it was transported and to some degree transformed to fit the Anglo-American critical tradition by Jonathan Culler, whose principle work was his *Structuralist Poetics* (1975). Culler built upon the New Criticism tradition, but purported to go beyond it by transcending mere interpretation. In his admirable essay entitled "Beyond Interpretation," in his book on *The Pursuit of Signs*, he deplores as effectively perhaps as anyone the fact that literary criticism has sunk to the level of mere interpretation, and he uses the examples of Christopher Frye and Stanley Fish, among vast numbers of other possibilities, to demonstrate how thoroughly consumed modern criticism is with interpretation, and how mere interpretation as an end of criticism will bring criticism to an end.

But as the leading spokesman for structuralism in the Anglo-American world Culler did not himself get much beyond the role of critic as interpreter, i.e., scholar, and in fact he insisted upon an even more rigorous scientific exploration of language than his European predecessors had done. He got bogged down in the pursuit of "signs," and he certainly did not do anything to stem the twentieth century process of trivializing literature.

But as it turned out, the structuralists did not have the last word on the impact of the scientific method upon language. That task was left to the post-structuralists, and specifically the phenomenon of deconstructionism. The post-structuralists agree with the structuralists that meaning is a construction produced by the arrangement of language or symbolic forms. But the post-structuralists deny that the arrangement can ever be systematic or even coherent. They do not believe that the author can really say what he means because the nature of language will not permit him to do so. They emphasize the inevitable difference between what the author intended to say and what he in fact did say. Words cannot be trusted to convey a universal meaning, and therefore if the reader is to get any meaning from a work he is going to have to create it himself. It is the reader, not the author who is important, and the reader's reading is more important than the writer's writings. The post-structuralist's job then is to emphasize the discontinuity between what is intended by the author and what is actually expressed. And since no system of language or symbol can accurately convey meaning, then every construction which employs language or symbols can be deconstructed. In a sense, then, the post-structuralists pulled the rug out from under the structuralists almost as soon as the structuralists stepped onto it.

The structuralists simply did not carry the scientizing of language far enough. They were naive in still believing that an objective meaning could be got out of a verbal structure. They did not perceive that if the scientific method were carried far enough that it would have to conclude that language is meaningless, that words are concepts, not percepts, and that there is no predictability of meaning in them. And yet predictability is the acid test of the scientific method, and certainly words are going to have different meanings for different readers, so that exactly the same reaction to words by all readers is impossible. If, for example, a novelist writes, "A dog was barking in the yard," the reader has no idea what kind of dog was barking, how the bark sounds or how the yard looks; the reader is left to his own peculiar imagination. And even if the novelist spends pages describing the dog and the bark and the yard—and in the process loses the thread of his narrative—the reader will still have to picture in his own peculiar way what the novelist had in mind, even though he may not have had enough in mind to say much more than that "A dog was barking in the yard." When an author's text becomes far more abstract and abstruse, then the levels of meaning, and indeed the meaning itself as well as the problem of communication, become infinitely more complex.

But the post-structuralists go much farther. They insist that words in fact get in the way of reality. Words rely upon other words for their meaning, and other words, which are also remote from reality, make the word they try to define even more remote from reality. This is the conclusion that the post-structuralists came to, and they were thus left only with the necessity of demonstrating the impossibility that any writer can accurately communicate with words. They are thus in a position to deny the fundamental premise of the structuralists that consistent meaning is possible and can therefore be investigated. They do not believe that any arrangement of words can be systematic or coherent. They deny too that the reader can ever be detached, so that the solipsistic reader and the slippery meaning of words render any kind of objective meaning impossible.

The inevitable conclusion of their premises is that the text can have no meaning or else that it can have any meaning that the reader wants to attach to it, but it is his own private meaning, and will be as wrong or as right as any other reader's meaning.

Like the structuralists, the post-structuralists had their origin in France, this time under the guidance of Jacques Derrida. Derrida's now famous dictum that *"Il n'y a rien hors du texte,"* which is perhaps best translated as "There is no outside-the-text," indicates his insistence that there is no relationship between the text and reality. He does not deny reality; he simply denies that the text in any way represents reality, specifically objective reality. As a philosopher he first applied the theory in order to "deconstruct" Western metaphysics, but almost at once the principle was picked up by literary critics who proceeded to deconstruct literary texts or rather to show how literary texts deconstruct themselves.

I do not wish to simplify the concept of deconstruction, because it cannot be simplified. The works of Derrida are astoundingly difficult, and furthermore the major exponents of the movement disagree even on many major points. Professor Richard Rorty, a major representative of the movement in the United States, once observed that "Even God probably doesn't know what it means to deconstruct a text." For example, Michael Foucault, the historian, and Jacques Lacan, the psychoanalyst, and Roland Barthes, the literary critic, are often at serious odds with one another over the process of deconstructing a text. But in general they agree that what is important is not what the writer writes but how the reader reads, and even that is not important because how the reader reads produces no more understanding of reality than what the writer writes.

Derrida himself spread his doctrine of deconstructionism in person on both the East Coast and the West Coast, and his teachings have now filled much of the university space in between. American scholars who were slow to accept structuralism despite the efforts of Jonathan Culler and a few others, fell, as they say, hook, line, and sinker, for deconstructionism. In fact Derrida himself observed that deconstructionism was "stronger in the United States than anywhere else." And since that time it has been growing still stronger, even while interest in the movement has experienced a major falling off in

Europe itself. American intellectuals in fact have become so mesmerized by the whole idea of deconstructionism that they have become more and more pre-occupied with literary theory than with literature itself. One of the consequences of the rise of deconstructionism is that literary criticism has been made to seem more important and more interesting in some quarters than the literature it tries to deconstruct. The movement has not only rendered literature and literary criticism indistinguishable; it has elevated, indeed exalted, literary criticism above the literature which it is supposed to serve; so that it is possible to conclude that deconstructionism is really a means of self-aggrandizement. Matthew Arnold had insisted that the creative faculty is higher than the critical faculty. The deconstructionists would reverse the order.

American intellectuals have been hard at work extending the implications of the premises of post-structuralism further than had been done in Europe. The idea that words have no objective meaning has been applied to virtually all disciplines which deal with words and symbols, and hence has influenced not only literature and literary criticism, but philosophy, religion, anthropology, history, and potentially every other recognized discipline. It has even, ironically enough, begun to be applied to science itself, with the possible eventual results of undermining the validity of even the pure sciences and hence the scientific method since numbers are as much abstractions as words, and hence subject to the same charge of having no relationship to objective reality.

Deconstructionism has become a weapon for anyone who wants to attack the writings of anyone else, and there is no telling where the influence will end. Some observers say that interest in post-structuralism in America is dying because it keeps coming up against common sense and common experience, while others believe that it has already become a permanent part of intellectual history in America.

Whoever is right, it has to be evident that even though the deconstructionists may be temporarily the winners, literature itself is the loser. To face the charge that poems and plays and stories have no objective meaning is the greatest of the many blows which literature has yet been dealt by literary theorists and critics. The deconstructionists have come not to praise literature, but to bury it. And yet, however short-lived their influence may be, they still represent, if not the mainstream of intellectual history, at least a consequential tributary. The primary force behind post-structuralism is the scientific spirit, which inevitably was going to be applied to language, and with the inevitable outcome of attempting to destroy its efficacy as a means of communicating truth and reality.

*****

The fourth and so far final stage in the development of literary theory and criticism in this saga of the trivialization of literature was created by those who politicize literature. One of the reasons that the literary politicizors are so formidable is that, unlike their predecessors in the nineteenth and twentieth centuries, they are able to define—and with a vengeance—just what the purpose of literature is. That purpose is quite simply political. Politicizors disdain, indeed are contemptuous of, the romantic concept of literature, which is merely self-expression, and the hedonistic view that literature provides merely a moment of pleasure. In addition, they reject the formalist critics with their pre-occupation with the form of a literary work to the exclusion of its external influences and values. They also, theoretically, reject the deconstructionist view that language in general is meaningless, though that has not prevented them from deconstructing literary works which are contrary to their own political preferences. Instead, for them the purpose of literature is to promote certain political values and ideologies which they themselves embrace and which they are convinced everyone should embrace, usually ideologies of the radical left. Like a good many earlier critical theorists, they plunder literary works for their extra-literary values, not as repositories of myths or symbols or psychoanalytical or anthropological value, but for their political ideology. In thinking of literature in this way they are able to transform their political zeal into literary zeal by the prospect that certain literary works will lend support to their political orientation. Politicizing literary theorists think of literature as a powerful tool to transform society into a political utopia. Literature, they believe, can lead the way to a more just and equitable and in general a happier society. It can help political dreamers realize a vision.

It is important to make the distinction here between political literature and the politicizing of literature. Political literature, i.e., plays and poems and stories which are written more or less with the aim of advancing a political position is as old as the Greeks and can be found in the literature of almost all ages. Even Shakespeare's history plays recommend a rather broad political position. The politicizing of literature, on the other hand, seeks to plunder literature in order to pluck out support for a particular political or social ideology regardless of what the author actually intended. Basically the difference is that political literature consists of the creation of poets, dramatists, and fiction writers, whereas the politicizing of literature is the creation of literary critics. The authors of political literature use literature to dignify politics; political critics use politics to dignify literature. Both distort the highest purpose of literature; political literature however can still be good literature, but the politicizing of literature, as we shall see, can never be good criticism.

I should like briefly to trace the rise of political criticism and to suggest something of the way in which it is in reality one more blow to the dignity and prestige of the literary arts, to suggest that the politcizors of literature end up selling literature as short as the critical theorists already described. I begin with a brief consideration of Marxist criticism, which is the grand source of political criticism, and which supplied the examples, if not the models for subsequent efforts to politicize literature.

In some sense it may be said that Marxist criticism grew out of the nineteenth century tradition of historical critics, such as Hippolyte Taine, who employed an historical perspective as a means of understanding literary texts and also as a means of understanding history. Nineteenth century political criticism in the Taine tradition was often a disinterested inquiry, though it had strong relativistic and deterministic overtones. Marxist critics, however, developed their own peculiar historical dialectic which caused them to examine literature through an ideological overlay, specifically a Marxist overlay; and when they did, they saw, often very quickly, whether a literary work fit or did not fit into the Marxist mold. Marxist literary theory in its purest form uses literature as a tool to promote Marxist ideology, and it elevates works that do and denigrates works that don't, regardless of the relative artistic value of the literature. It thus has a handy guide for determining whether a piece of literature is "good" or "bad." Its criteria are not primarily or broadly moral, but narrowly political and social and economic in accordance with the Marxist world view.

Karl Marx himself illustrates perhaps as well as anyone the politicizing of literature and the shifting away from the aesthetic and broadly moral purpose of literature. Dickens, Thackeray, Charlotte Brontë, and Mrs. Gaskell, he declared, "have issued to the world more political and social truths than have been uttered by all the professional politicians, publicists, and moralists put together." His observations suggest what Marxist critics in fact do, namely plunder literature for its extra-literary values, for its evidence of the truth of Marxist socialist and political doctrine.

What Marxist critics do, then, is pounce upon literature of social protest as evidence of the rightness of Marxism, and they disparage literature which seeks to understand the mere universal and spiritual nature of mankind. Terry Eagleton, an American exponent of Marxist criticism, observes that "from Percy Bysshe Shelley to Norman N. Holland, literary theory has been indissociably bound up with political beliefs and ideological values. Indeed literary theory is less an object of intellectual inquiry in its own right than a particular perspective in which to view the history of our time." Actually, it is more nearly true to say that Marxist critics have themselves made literary theory "indissociably bound up" with political and ideological values, specifically Marxist beliefs and values.

Those who followed the Soviet literary scene where Marxist criticism has prevailed may perceive how narrowly the purpose of literature was pursued. In the Soviet Union novelists and poets and dramatists who conformed to the dictates of "Socialist Realism" (which prescribed the rules that Soviet writers had to follow in order to make Communism a convincing system) were rewarded with public honors, a better apartment, and a car. Those who disobeyed the rules of Socialist Realism by writing about the dignity of the individual and about the problems and aspirations of mankind without reference to socialist values were exiled, imprisoned, or executed, or at the very least run out of the Soviet Writers Union, even though the aesthetic and moral value of the works, of such writers as Pasternak, Anna Akhmatova, Shevchenko, Isaac Babel, and numerous others is far superior to that of most of those who received the blessing of the Soviet government.

In a free world, however, Marxist critics can only suggest and propose and plead in a society where everyone else is allowed to do the same. Partly in order to avoid the stigma of the crude critical theory of Marxism which grew out of the 1920s and 30s, Marxist critics beginning with George Lucacs, Granville Hicks, onward to include Raymond Williams in England, and Fredric Jameson, Hayden White, and others in America, have so subtlized Marxist criticism that sometimes it appears to be hardly Marxist at all. This phenomenon has allowed greater credence to Marxist criticism and hence a greater influence. But the fundamental premise remains the same: using literature as a tool to build a socialist state and a socialist culture and to destroy the capitalist system and a capitalist culture. With that criterion as a guide, they stretch, yank, squash, and chop literary works until they fit into the procustean bed of Marxism. The warping and twisting and molding of the works of writers as diverse as Dickens, Shelley, Charlotte Brontë, and Mark Twain, to name a few, exemplify their true aim.

Yet Marxist criticism has a vitality that the New Criticism and the other forms of literary scholarship which pass for literary criticism do not. Marxists have good reasons to feel strongly about literature because they feel strongly about the political aims of Marxism. The political respect for the power of literature, carried to its extreme, may be exemplified in the critical theory of the late Ayatollah Khomeini, who put a price on the heads of authors whose works he did not like.

In recent years there has developed another school of political criticism, now widely known as the New Historicism. Many of the proponents of this movement are careful to distance themselves from the Marxist critics, but their aims and methods are often startlingly similar. They profess to be reacting to the narrowness of the formalist school with its obsession with the details of language and form to the exclusion of any reference outside the literary work, especially to the social and political milieu with which they themselves are pre-occupied. The New Historicists ostensibly aim to restore the importance of what an author is saying, particularly on a political level, and in practice often end up, like the Marxist critics, judging the value of a literary work more by its politics than its artistic excellence. Under the guise of careful scholarship they ferret out works dating back to the Middle Ages and Renaissance in order to find a justification for their own political convictions. Basically the New Historicism proceeds on the assumption that nothing can be learned from history, that no modern reader can really understand a literary work written in its own milieu, that it does not deal with universal truth but merely with truths that were true only for the time in which it was written. Thus, since a Renaissance literary work, for example, has meaning only for the Renaissance, then it must be treated not as a work of art but as an historical document. No single culture or literature therefore may be said to be superior to any other. The New Historicist tends to deny the transcendent value of literature or the universal value of literature, on the assumption that one age cannot really communicate with another age. But the way that past literature can serve the present, they believe, is to regard it as a repository of ideologies which have meaning for our time. The idea, then, is to seek them out through diligent scholarship and identify them and to recommend them to the twentieth century.

The problem that is raised at once, however, is whether the New Historicists are not imposing their own ideologies on the literature of the past and hence whether they are not using substantially the same methods as Marxist critics in misreading the aims and philosophical premises of any literary work under study. One can imagine, for example, what New Historicists do to Shakespeare's works. One New Historicist finds that Iago's plot against Othello represents the standard Elizabethan attempt to deny "the otherness of subject peoples." There seems no doubt but that the New Historicism in general represents a far-left-of-center plundering of supposed ideologies or philosophical premises in literary texts in the name of scholarship and history.

One scholar, D. G. Myers in "The New Historicism in Literary Studies," (in *Academic Questions,* 1988-9, p. 32) points out that anyone who reads widely in the New Historicists find that their writings turn primarily upon what he calls "*au courant* sympathy for exploited peoples, powerless women, workers, slaves, and peasants." But the problem is not the concern of the New Historicists for the downtrodden, which is not a problem; the problem is the way in which they use literature merely for their own ideological ends, and in this way they are not remarkably different from the Marxist critics.

Even though the movement did not begin to make itself felt until the early 1980s, it has already made major inroads in the nation's colleges and universities. It has its own journal *Representations*, its own guru, Stephen Greenblatt, and an increasingly large number of devoted followers both in American and English universities But the central fact is that the New Historicists, by denigrating not only the aesthetic but the universal moral value of literature in order to concentrate on its real or imagined ideological value, make their own peculiar contribution to the trivializing of literature, which has become the characteristic feature of most twentieth century critical theory.

Another major movement in the direction of politicizing literature, and one which in the long run may be more significant than either the Marxist or the New Historicist critics is that professed by feminist critics. Feminist criticism pleads the rightful cause of a proper and just representation of women in literature. It begins with the insistence that women in literature have been badly portrayed because the writers have been men and therefore bring with them the ancient cultural attitudes and prejudices against women. In short, women at the hands of literary men have been represented as inferior not only physically, but spiritually, morally, intellectually, artistically, socially, emotionally, and in just about every other way that women have widely suffered from a masculine view of them. Second, men, until recently, have succeeded so well in keeping women from developing their intellects and talents that they have not had an opportunity even to write, much less to portray other women the way they should be portrayed. Feminist critics are properly pleased to argue that educated women were so rare in the past that they didn't begin to make their literary voices felt in any consequential way until the nineteenth century, and then often amidst jeers and sneers despite the achievements of writers like Jane Austen, the Brontë sisters, George Eliot, and a handful of others who demonstrate an undoubted literary genius. When Charlotte Brontë, for example, wrote Robert Southey for his opinion of her work, he replied that "literature is not the business of a woman's life, and it cannot be." And when she did publish her novels it was under a man's name.

But gradually women did begin to make great gains in education, and by the middle of the twentieth century enough of them had done so that they could not only demonstrate literary talent which challenges that of most men writers but could effectively rebel against the shabby treatment they had endured throughout history both in literature and life. In the forefront of this crusade were Virginia Woolf and Simone de Beauvoir, who may be regarded as pioneers in women's intellectual challenge to a male-dominated culture, Virginia Woolf most of all in *A Room of One's Own* and Simone de Beauvoir in *The Second Sex*. The influence of their work encouraged the development of a feminist literary criticism and a feminist aesthetic.

The movement is now being led by a group of young and not-so-young angry women, most of whom are professors of literature in universities across the country, and include such outspoken women as Elaine Showalter, Sandra Gilbert, Susan Gubar, Annette Kolodny, and Lillian S. Robinson among others. They write about literature with a zeal and a conviction which exponents of the fact-seeking school of criticism cannot approach because, like the Marxists and more recently the New Historicists, they know, or think they know, what the purpose of literature ought to be, and they therefore sharpen their critical instincts by exposing the "bad" literature and exalting the "good"; the "bad" being literature, mostly by men, who misrepresent women, and the "good" literature, mostly by women, which does not misrepresent them, or which represents them in the way they think they should be represented.

As a result of this zeal feminist critics have made themselves felt on the literary scene; they have succeeded in resurrecting the reputations of some minor nineteenth century women authors, and their viewpoint is widely represented in the programs of the annual Modern Language Association conventions. They are also busily employed in altering the literary canon in the colleges not only by teaching courses in women's literature, and indeed women's studies, but by attempting to displace literary works by men with literary works by women. They are, in short, a force to be reckoned with, and they support a cause far more noble than that of the Marxists or the New Historicists.

Like the Marxists and the New Historicists, however, their criteria for determining the value of a literary work is not aesthetic and broadly moral. It is the degree of "correctness" in the representation of women in a literary work which determines its worth, just as the Marxists look primarily for degrees of social and political orthodoxy. Feminist criticism is thus another form of the politicizing of literature, and feminist critics readily acknowledge the fact. In Professor Showalter's view, for example, "the feminist critique is essentially political and polemical." And there is no doubt but that feminist critics are using literature as a weapon to advance feminist interests just as Marxist critics and the New Historicists use literature to advance far-left interests.

It may be, however, that the most zealous of the feminist literary critics are doing their cause more harm than good. Some feminist critics, it is true, have grown less strident and more thoughtful, just as most Marxist critics have done, in order to give their theories greater credence. But in many instances too they have taken an adversarial stance by pitting women's literature against men's literature, a kind of he-said she-said duality, and they may in effect be turning the study of literature into a battle of the sexes. The publication of the *Norton Anthology of Women's literature* (1984) suggests that there is a women's literature as well as a men's literature, just as there is herstory as well as history. Nonetheless the flood of first-rate women writers now appearing on the scene makes their case all the more compelling.

The arrival of women's studies has led to a whole new phenomenon on American campuses, a phenomenon which might be called the "studies movement, "which is now sheltered under the broad tent of "multiculturalism."

Multiculturalism implies the study of the cultures of minorities, so that in a sense "women's studies" do not constitute a minority, but rather a majority, including the fact that more women now attend college than men, and worldwide they are not in any sense a minority. In fact, "women's studies" constitute a far greater group of "studies" than any other on the multicultural menu. In the 1960s, however, the rise of "black studies" or "Afro-American studies" provided the pattern for a whole series of more recent studies, including American Indian studies, Asian-American studies, Chicano/Chicana studies, Latino/Latina studies, Puerto Rican studies, gay-and-lesbian studies, and even, as if in self-defense, "men's studies." There are others too and more are likely to appear. Many of these "studies" have already developed into interdisciplinary programs, but I do not wish here to further differentiate among them, except to make a few general observations about the phenomenon so far as their impact upon the well-being of the literary arts is concerned.

In their most virulent form, these studies, including women's studies, have as their chief enemy what has come to be called the "dead, white male." This term has implications not only for literature but for other disciplines also, especially history, for it implies an attack not only upon the history of Western Civilization, and hence of the past in general, going all the way back to the classical Greeks, but upon the whole literary heritage of Western Civilization, all the way back to Homer, and all the others of the greatest writers of the past since, desirable or not, they have virtually all been men and dead and white. These studies mean, then, a cutting off of the past because most of these minorities do not have a significant literary past. Thus, insofar as these studies begin to dominate the college curricula, the literary heritage of Western Civilization will be lost, and in fact is being lost.

A second problem with the studies movement is that it plays havoc with any attempt to preserve a literary canon because each party in the studies movement promotes its own literary works, usually at the expense of the greatest literary works of Western Civilization, which are being increasingly pushed out of the curriculum to make way for whatever minority literature each studies program puts forward, so that any literary canon at all becomes difficult to preserve. Furthermore, an underlying assumption of the studies movement is that no culture is inferior to any other culture, and that since they are all equal, regardless of how limited the literary value of their literature may be, it appears that the final result will be no generally acknowledged literary heritage to inherit because each group of students under each studies program will have studied literary works wholly unknown to any other group of students. It may be, therefore, that we may in time reach a point at which there is cause to rejoice that any literature at all is taught in college, regardless of which minority has produced it.

*****

I have tried, then, in this chapter to highlight the development of literary theories and literary criticism which would appear not to be in the best interests of the literary arts, especially the high literary arts, and to indicate how they are being transmitted or not transmitted to the next generation. The loss has been very great, and is in a fair way to becoming even greater. There are many, even in high educational places, who do not, or will not, mourn the loss, and I therefore propose in Chapter V of this study to indicate something of the nature of that loss, not so much, perhaps, to convince the long string of literary theorists and critics who have contributed to the trivializing of literature, but to reassure those who still recognize and cherish the idea that literature is, as Sir Philip Sidney put it, "the highest form of earthly learning." Meanwhile, these threats to the thriving, even the surviving of literature, along with others, are not only in the minds of literary theorists but are practiced, sometimes with a vengeance, in the classrooms of the nation's schools and colleges and universities, and I will try to outline them in the next two chapters.

Chapter III

Phasing Out Literature
in American Education

The last chapter called attention to the monumental irony that the literary theorists, who ought to defend the literary arts, have, for the past hundred years, been busy inventing theories which trivialize literature and in recent decades which even undertake to destroy its authority utterly. But the schools and universities, in part under the influence of the literary theorists, constitute a more serious threat to the future of literature than the literary theorists themselves.

The literary theorists deal in such rarified speculations and abstractions, often in nearly unintelligible language, that they sometimes appear to be so far removed from reality that they are automatically rendered harmless. But as I have tried to indicate they cannot be dismissed so easily because they are the products of the mainstream of intellectual history in the Western World; and their influence, though subtle, could conceivably be profound and longlasting.

There is no arguing, on the other hand, the enormous influence of the education system in determining whether students inherit their literary heritage and whether they will develop a genuine respect for literature, if not a love for it. If students do not get a good literary education in the schools and colleges, they very likely won't get it at all.

Before examining the nature of the threat of the American education system to the future of literature, however, I should like for a moment to take a brief but broad look at the general curriculum in American schools, because it will, I believe, help explain what has happened to the teaching of literature.

The curriculum of the schools and colleges of any country tends to provide a highly accurate reflection of its cultural values. The so-called core requirements of the curriculum, whether at the elementary and secondary level or the college level, offer a particularly clear measure of the values which a nation holds dear, not only what students are required to study, but what they are not required to study.

The curriculum of American schools and colleges seems to be a particularly accurate measure of American cultural values, and it tends to be widely at variance with the curriculum of the schools of both Western and Eastern Europe, and of Japan. What most clearly distinguishes the curriculum of the American system of education from that of virtually every other highly civilized country in the world is the relative freedom from serious study of the traditional disciplines: history, literature, geography, mathematics, the sciences, and foreign languages. Some students, of course, do get substantial exposure to at least some of these disciplines, especially at the private schools and some suburban schools, but few students in general get extensive exposure to more than to one or two, and oftentimes not to any of the major disciplines at all. It is widely recognized, for example, that in the schools history and geography tend to get buried in a "social studies" curriculum, which sometimes includes almost everything except history and geography. Mathematics and the sciences are usually highly diluted in the elementary schools and are even phased out for many students in the high schools, particularly the laboratory sciences. Most students do not study a foreign language, or if they do, they do so for only one or two years, and then in such a fashion that not more than two or three percent of them come away from high school with anything like a competent knowledge of it. It is not necessary to demonstrate the truth of these charges here; it is possible to call upon study after study, both government and private, which confirm anyone's worst fears about how ill-taught most high school graduates are in any of the basic disciplines, and even a college degree no longer provides any assurance that the colleges have necessarily achieved what the schools have not. The authoritative study of the National Committee on Excellence in Education entitled *A Nation at Risk* concluded that "for the first time in the history of our country, the educational skills of one generation will not surpass, will not equal, will not even approach those of their parents."

At the university level, something of the falloff in the teaching of the fundamental disciplines is reflected in a 1996 report by the National Association of Scholars, which is represented by some 3,500 academics, who are alarmed by the dilution and politization of higher education. It is entitled "The Dissolution of General Education: 1914-1993," and points out that of 50 elite colleges and universities studied, 90 percent of them in 1964 had requirements in the biological and physical sciences, whereas in 1993 only 34 percent did. In 1964 as much as 90 percent of them had a foreign language requirement, but in 1993 only 64 percent did; and in 1964 history courses were required at 60 percent of the institutions but by 1993 only 2 percent were. And most pertinent to this study, in 1964 as much as 50 percent had a literature requirement, but in 1993 zero percent did.

In so anti-intellectual an atmosphere, therefore, it is not possible to expect that the role of literature will typically assume any great importance in the curriculum of most colleges and universities, and indeed it does not. There are two separate, yet related phenomena which prevent students from learning much literature, much less acquiring any respect for it. The first is the high incidence of illiteracy and semi-literacy, and the other is the loss of any kind of literary canon which would enable students to read the best literature and to properly admire it.

I should like first to make a few observations about the problem of illiteracy in the United States. At the present time the United States ranks 49th among 158 United Nations members in its level of illiteracy, three times that of Russia and five times that of Cuba. The schools must not be allowed to hide behind the argument—as most educators do—that they turn out so many illiterates and semi-literates because there are so many minorities and dropouts. In October 1985, according to a General Accounting Office study, there were about 4.3 million dropouts nationally, ages 16 to 24, but about 3.5 million of these were white, only 700,000 black, and 100,000 from other races. Furthermore if students are properly taught, they should be good readers long before they are allowed to drop out at age 16. They should be pretty good readers by the end of the third grade, and very good readers by the end of the sixth grade. Sixth graders ought to be able to read the very widely used sixth grade McGuffey reader of the last century or the equivalent of the sixth grade reader in the Russian schools, the Japanese schools, or the equivalent of the sixth grade reader in virtually any of the schools of continental Europe. But most of them cannot. Following, for example, is an excerpt from the fifth grade McGuffey Reader, from a series which sold more than 120 million copies between 1836 and 1920, and hence were more widely used than any other series during that period. It is an excerpt from Charles Dickens' *Nicholas Nickleby:*

> Pale and haggard faces, lank and bony figures, children with the countenances of old men, deformities with irons upon their limbs, boys of stunted growth, and others whose long, meager legs would hardly bear their stooping bodies, all crowded on the view together. There were little faces which should have been handsome, darkened with the scowl of sullen, dogged suffering. There was childhood with the lights of its eye quenched, its beauty gone, and its helplessness alone remaining.

A passage from a sixth grade reader, widely used in the Catholic schools in the nineteenth century, entitled *The Young Catholic's School Series* (1880) would be far more intimidating. The opening sentences of the first lesson entitled "An Exhortation to the Study of Eloquence," are as follows:

> I cannot conceive anything more excellent than to be able, by language, to captivate the affections, to charm the understanding, and to impel or restrain the will of whole assemblies at pleasure. Among every free people, especially in peaceful, settled governments, this single art has always eminently flourished, and exercised the greatest sway.

Apart from the unfamiliar sentiments, very few students in contemporary American schools either at the fifth or the sixth grade level would likely come anywhere close to being able to read this passage with its literate vocabulary and relatively sophisticated style. Neither, it is safe to say, could many modern high school seniors. Clearly, the intent of nineteenth century and early twentieth century American schools was to make students fully literate by the end of the sixth grade. The simple and banal selections of a typical American sixth grade reader with its meager vocabulary provides the best evidence of the plunge in reading standards, which do not require a former level of sixth grade reading skills until at least the tenth grade, by which time a fairly large percentage of students have already dropped out of school. The United States is not a nation of dunces. American students are as intellectually capable as those of any other nation's students. They can be taught to read as well as students in any other country, and they are potentially as good readers whether they represent minorities or not. The fact is that most of those who cannot read English or read it badly, speak English natively and are products of our schools.

The conclusion would be, then, that if students who go through at least the eighth grade of our schools cannot read and read well, the fault lies not with the parents or the parents' plight, or the students or the students' plight, or the environment or the electronic revolution or any other potential enemy of the written page, but with the schools themselves. The problem lies specifically with the elementary schools, and more specifically the first three grades, because if students have not learned to read well by the end of the third grade, they will very likely never learn to read well. These pristine years are ideal for teaching students to read. During the first three grades students are docile, pliable, and normally eager to learn; they do not yet use drugs or hard liquor, nor are many of them yet juvenile delinquents. The only legitimate excuses of the schools in failing to teach students to read in these grades is the genuinely dyslexic student, the seriously disturbed student, the retarded student, or the student whose native language is not English. Such students make up only a small fraction of students who cannot read well.

Nor does the fact that some students come from illiterate or semi-literate homes constitute a sufficient excuse. During the first three grades students do not have to read many words that are not already in their speaking vocabulary no matter how small it may be, and there is nothing to prevent them in the next three grades from learning words which are not in their speaking vocabulary.

The full burden of teaching students to read must fall upon the schools. The constant cry from education authorities that the parents must help out at home is merely a symptom of how badly the schools are failing in making students literate.

It will be clear enough that the future of literature in America depends above all on the future of literacy; and wherever literacy, genuine literacy, is not acquired, the future of literature is at risk. Some observations, then, are in order which will perhaps help explain why American schools turn out so many semi-literates compared to those of any other economically advanced country.

The chief answer must be sought in the methods of teaching reading which have dominated the elementary schools in America for the past forty years and which is about the time that the literacy rate began to fall. The single most important cause of semi-literacy in the schools comes from abandoning in the 1940s the phonics approach to reading in favor of what came to be called the look-say method. The phonics method teaches the student the sounds of all the letters and letter combinations in English by the end of the first semester of the first grade, if not before. It is the method used in virtually all the schools worldwide with alphabetical languages. It takes its logic from the fact that the letters stand for sounds, and that if a student knows the sounds of the letters he can usually determine what the word means—even without help, especially if the word is already in his speaking vocabulary, which in the first few grades it generally is. It is overwhelmingly the common-sense approach to reading for all languages with an alphabet. It was used universally in the American school system from its inception until about 1940.

The shift to the look-say method came about because leading pedagogues concluded that students can learn to read more quickly by memorizing the design of the word on the page and by other non-phonics tricks, much as a student can learn to play the piano quickly by memorizing which keys to hit without learning to read music. The revolution is epitomized by Nela Bantam Smith in a pamphlet ironically entitled *Sailing into Reading*, as past president of the likewise ironically titled International Reading Association (IRA) and widely distributed by the National Education Association (NEA), another ironic title. The advent of look-say, said Smith, has doomed the alphabet "as decisively as the wooden clipper was doomed by the steel-bottomed ships. Why teach the child an artificial method of looking at each letter when, in life's reading, he recognizes one word from another by its total shape and unique characteristics." In the long run, however, the method doesn't work because the non-phonics tricks which are instilled in the student are vastly less reliable than the phonics method, and they leave him with no way to learn to read words on his own. And it has a disastrous effect upon his ability to spell. Most schools today have backed off from the anti-phonics spirit of the IRA and NEA in the 1940s and now introduce students to the sounds of the letters, bit by bit, sometimes over a period of three years. In many cases they are denied the full phonics facts until it is too late.

Advocates of the look-say, or better described as the look-and-guess method, also point out that English is not a very phonetic language and that the student can thus easily by tricked by it. That argument is not valid either because all alphabetical languages are highly phonetic by definition, though some are somewhat more phonetic than others; and no language is perfectly phonetic.

Perhaps the main point to be made here is that, despite decades of controversy as to whether the phonics or the look-say, or versions thereof, is superior, the advocates of look-say have so far won out that there is not a single phonics program widely used in the public schools, though several are on the market. The phonics method is almost entirely confined to select private and suburban schools. As a result, almost all the so-called basic reading series introduce students to only about three or four hundred words a year for the first three years, which is about a fourth or fifth of the number of words that they are capable of learning if they are taught by a systematic phonics method. And since they have not been taught the habit of "sounding out" words from the beginning, millions of them are handicapped for life because they soon get in over their heads as the textbooks become increasingly difficult. In fact, it has been necessary to scale down—or dumb down, as the expression goes—the degree of difficulty of textbooks by often as much as two years, and sometimes more, because of the crippling effect of the look-say method of teaching reading. The NEA and IRA support an anti-phonics stance even more belligerently now than they did forty years ago, and their influence will do much to prevent any consequential reduction in the vast numbers of illiterates and semi-literates whom the schools turn out every year.

In recent years, however, the reading specialists in the schools of Education across the country have invented an even more nightmarish pedagogical approach which is generally known as the "whole language" method. This practice places before the student some literature of a higher quality than that of the Dick-and-Jane era, but still avoids a systematic phonics approach. Instead the students are invited to guess at a word from its context, often with not a clue as to how the letters of the word sound. Furthermore they are invited to skip over the words that they can't figure out. The rationale for this approach is that it introduces students more or less at once to interesting readings, and thereby allows students to avoid the temporary annoyance of having to learn how the letters of the words sound.

The preposterousness of this approach has become particularly poignant in the California schools, which lent its considerable influence in spreading the "whole language" method to other parts of the country. But while this method was being practiced in California over a period of the last five or six years, California schools saw students' reading scores plummet until they were tied for last place along with Louisiana. Governor Pete Wilson was so embarrassed by student performance that he offered to pay schools to teach systematic phonics and to support the re-education of elementary school teachers who had not learned how to teach phonics but were well-versed in "whole language" techniques. Thus the whole problem of the best method of teaching reading has become politicized. The reading authorities of California and of other states have understandably resisted the common-sense intensive phonics approach because after almost a half-century they have developed a reflex reaction against it. And still the battle rages on, but it has become so crucial to the education of students that it is no longer a controversy to be fought out by the educational establishment within university walls, but has been pushed into the political arena, where politicians usually take no interest in pedagogical problems. Just how far a nationwide movement toward a restoration of systematic phonics will get is still problematical, given the instinctive opposition to it in elementary school pedagogical circles.

*****

The first of the two great threats of the American education system to the literary arts, then, is the failure of the schools to make large numbers of students fully literate. The second of the great threats to the future of literature stemming from our education system is the failure to maintain a literary canon, a body of literature which can be regarded as the student's literary heritage, both of our own country and of the world.

To speak in broad terms about preserving the literary heritage of Western Civilization in the Christian era, it was the medieval monasteries which first recognized the need to preserve the great literature of the past, and which at the time consisted chiefly of whatever major Greek and Latin literature was known and whatever important literature had accrued during the early centuries of Christianity. This role of preserving the literature of Western Civilization was passed on to the universities in the later Middle Ages and to the Latin grammar schools of the Renaissance, both in England and on the continent. In the Renaissance particularly, students were brought up on the Greek and especially the Latin classics, while at the same time they were mastering the Latin and often trying to master the Greek language. To be sure, it was a narrow canon. Basically, they all studied much the same works with special emphasis upon Cicero, Virgil, and Horace as the core of their studies.

The systematic study of vernacular literatures and languages in the schools did not come about until well into the nineteenth century. But the point is that during these centuries there was a general recognition that there was a body of literature which all students ought to study, on the grounds that such literature represented the best that had been thought and said in the world. Not the least of the advantages of the preservation of a literary canon was that all students enjoyed a common literary ground which enabled them to communicate in a common language. Even American schools recognized that grade school students all ought to be taught a common body of literature, the general nature of which was largely agreed upon. The nineteenth century McGuffey Readers indicate that by at least the fourth grade, students ought to be introduced to some of the agreed upon works of literature that children their age ought to now. Such schools did much to guarantee that students inherit their literary heritage. For example, the fifth grade McGuffey reader quoted earlier in this chapter contains selections by numerous writers who even today, among well-educated circles, are widely recognized, a few of whom are Oliver Goldsmith, Robert Southey, Whittier, Leigh Hunt, Longfellow, Hawthorne, Irving, Tennyson, Thoreau, Thackeray, Charles Lamb, Bret Harte, and Shakespeare. The Catholic sixth grade reader referred to earlier contains selections by numerous writers well known also even now, including Goethe, Shakespeare, Burke, Hazlitt, Cervantes, Macaulay, Hugo, Cicero, Samuel Johnson, Dryden, Scott, and some forty other widely known authors. Similarly in the high schools in the early decades of the twentieth century one of the most popular literature texts was *From Beowulf to Thomas Hardy,* which, as the title suggests, consisted of selections which, it was generally agreed, were worthy to represent the entire range of the literary heritage of the English-speaking world.

In general, then, it may be said that from the Renaissance onward, both in Europe and later in America, literature in the schools was regarded as an important part of a student's education, and he was given more than a taste of the best literature that had been written in English. There was also something like general agreement on which literature, or at least which authors, ought to be studied. This agreement gave them all a common cultural bond and a common cultural experience that was as important to their education as their study of mathematics or history or geography. The study of the history of children's literature will show that there grew up gradually a kind of canon of literature for children which consisted of fables, legends, classical myths, fairy tales, nursery rhymes, and a wide variety of poems and stories by well-known authors who wrote stories and poems for children. Many of them had seeped into elementary school readers of the earlier twentieth century, and were common in the elementary literature texts of European schools as well, on account of their artistic merit, and often their moral value, as for example, Aesop's fables. They were so well known that it was thought that they should be part of all children's literary education because they represented some of the best devices for teaching children to respect and love literature and to develop their aesthetic and moral sensibilities. Many of these stories and poems are still available in tradebook editions, though many of them are not nearly so readily available as they once were. This common heritage was a potent form of national and cultural cement, the loss of which is great.

*****

In twentieth century American schools, however, again about 1940, this bonding, this cultural cement began to crumble until, now, at the end of the twentieth century, it may be said to have collapsed. In the elementary schools it has been almost wiped out, and for two basic reasons: the first is tied to the peculiar method of trying to teach students to read by the look-say method, or the whole-language method, and the second is the advent of a philosophy of education, once known as "life adjustment" education, which has rendered the preservation of a children's literary canon meaningless.

　　The look-say method and other non-phonics techniques used in teaching reading in the elementary grades, particularly in the Dick-and-Jane era, virtually ruled out the inclusion of most of the well-known children's stories and poems because the method is so inefficient that, as I have indicated previously, students cannot handle more than 300 or 400 new words a year in each of the first three grades, which is why the vocabulary of Dick-and-Jane type American school readers is so impoverished compared to the McGuffey readers or comparable readers in continental Europe Furthermore, these words were commonly selected from prescribed word lists which contain only the most commonly used and least troublesome words in the English language, so that if a children's selection contains words not on the list it could not appear in the students' readers. An examination of virtually any widely used elementary reader series for the first three grades may not turn up a single recognizable selection. Poetry in particular has virtually disappeared from these readers, even through the sixth grade, and wherever it does appear it is likely to be by a free-verse poet largely unknown to the outside world. In Russian and East European countries and Western European countries too, as well as in the elementary schools of nineteenth century America, as we have seen, genuine literary selections, both in poetry and prose, abound. Some American elementary readers used in combination with the "whole language" method previously referred to may contain a somewhat higher literary value, but as I have indicated, students are not given the necessary phonics instruction to be able to read them with any great degree of competence.

But the peculiar theories of teaching reading in American schools were also supplemented by another peculiar theory, namely that the selections in school readers should no longer emphasize the timeless and the universal, but the timely and the topical, not the then and the there but the here and the now. In the 1940s educational theory developed the notion that its main role was to adjust students to "life," to stress the importance of contemporary living and to expose students to more of what they were getting outside of the classroom than to emphasize the larger truths of life, through good literature, such as they had been getting before. The way was thus paved for life-adjustment stories of no literary value written by authors with little literary talents, and for eliminating good literature by well-known authors who did not happen to deal with contemporary topics. The widespread ridicule of the Dick-and-Jane type textbooks forced publishers to disguise the names and change the content slightly. But no one should be fooled by such a move, for the techniques and the quality of the reading have in most cases not consequentially changed.

As a result, the readers and literature texts in the middle schools or junior high grades are generally written down by at least two grades on account of the inefficient reading instruction in the elementary grades. The editors of the literature textbooks in these grades cannot include literary selections of a high order or with any degree of sophistication or literary value even if they were inclined to do so. The sixth grade McGuffey reader contains better and more sophisticated writings and writers than virtually any junior high or middle school textbook now in use in the seventh, eighth, and ninth grades.

Many schools, it is true, still attempt to preserve a systematic study of serious literature at the high school level. Some schools, for example, require students to study a year's worth of American literature and another of English literature, and some include at least a semester of world literature. But these requirements are becoming increasingly rare. In some schools, these courses have become electives, so that the enrollments are often severely reduced; but more often than not, high schools have no such requirements, and have not had them for some time.

Generally speaking, the key to the extent to which a canon of literature is being preserved in the high schools is whether or not the course is organized around an *anthology* of literature, English, American, or world literature, or whether the textbooks consist of individual paperback books, sometimes chosen at the whim or peculiar tastes of the teacher. A good anthology has the overwhelming advantage of guaranteeing students the opportunity of reading some of the best works of the best authors, preferably with a chronological principle, in order to provide them with a much-needed but increasingly rare historical perspective. In the best schools this approach has been preserved, and hence a sense of the literary heritage is likewise preserved. In the last decade or two, however, there has been a growing hostility toward the anthology approach to literature, partly out of a sense that such an approach is too rigid, but also for a more compelling reason: The preservation of a traditional canon of literature has fallen prey to the increasing influence of the life-adjustment concept, which was instrumental in destroying anything like a literary canon in the upper elementary and middle school grades. This anti-historical spirit is chiefly a reflection of the idea of progress, the idea that newer is better and that what has been unknown is better than what is already known. The influence of the scientific spirit is in good part responsible for the decreasing interest in the historical approach to almost everything, and for the increasing belief, even among historians, that history does not have anything to teach us.

This spirit is certainly the main reason for the decline in the study of history in the schools and in the decreasing interest in the past in general. The past has, in fact, been virtually cut off in the curriculum of the schools. In general, the study of the past must be learned chiefly through history and through literature, but the historical study of literature is increasingly going the way of the study of history itself. Complaints are now common among college professors that students come to college without any sense of the past, and certainly without any sense of the chronology of the past (though not many university curricula do much to make up for the deficiency either).

In more and more high schools the practice is to give up the historical approach to literature and hence to abandon the historically oriented anthology in favor of approaches which at best chip away at the literary canon and at worst obliterate it. The substitution of the genre approach for the historical approach, even in some good high schools, is becoming increasingly common; but the genre approach in practice tends to eliminate some of the best literature in favor of inferior literature which merely fits the genre, and the rising popularity of a themes approach to literature is an even greater threat to the canon because oftentimes literary selections are chosen not because they are the best but because they fit into the themes, which in the new age of multiculturalism may now be even political. The artistic quality of the literary selections assigned to some high school students would make even the most incorrigible philistine shudder. Some literary works assigned to high school students do have a literary value, some of them with even great value; but they cannot compete overall with the multitude of literary works going all the way back to *Beowulf* or to Homer's epics, and if students do not read the standard classics in high schools, most of them will not study them at all, even, sorry to say, in the colleges and universities. No one denies that the canon of literature taught in the schools changes, and indeed it should change, but the prevailing practice causes many students to conclude that there is no literary heritage to inherit.

The abandonment of the serious study of serious literature began, then, first in the elementary grades, spread to the middle grades, and finally more and more to the senior high grades. It has held out longest in the colleges and universities, but here too the possibility of students inheriting their literary heritage is under siege. Radical steps have already been taken to downgrade the role of literature in the college curriculum, and more are in the offing.

The increased inability, for example, of college freshmen to comprehend the printed page has drastically reduced the literary content of the typical freshman English course, oftentimes to the zero point. This development is being reflected in the anthologies now designed for college freshmen. There was a time when such textbooks were full of challenging, highly artistic, and sophisticated selections from authors dating all the way back to the classical period and including some of the most widely read and most influential authors. But such textbooks are now hard to find. An example of one such text is *The Norton Reader*, which is still used in some of the better colleges and universities, but most freshman anthologies now consist of short, easy articles, as often as not drawn from contemporary periodicals, and though often written by competent writers, rarely can make any pretenses to real literary value and can make no pretensions whatsoever to being part of anybody's literary canon. The problem is not only that college freshmen in the main cannot understand genuine literary texts but that the colleges too have fallen prey to the influence of life-adjustment theories with their emphasis upon the contemporary and the topical.

An even more serious development is suggested in a report to Congress (September, 1988) by the National Endowment for the Humanities (NEH) which points out that 45 percent of the colleges and universities in this country award bachelor's degrees to students who do not have to take a single course in English or American literature. As the report suggests, this phenomenon is merely a symptom of the declining role which American colleges and universities are permitting the humanities to play in a student's education. It points out that 37 percent of the colleges and universities have no history requirement, that 62 percent have no philosophy requirement and that 77 percent have no foreign language requirement. The report also indicates that in the academic year 1965-66 one of every six college students was majoring in the humanities; in 1985-86. the figure was one in 16.

The universities are the chief repository of literary learning, for if it is not preserved there it will not be preserved anywhere. It is the last bastion, and increasingly the only bastion of the literary arts, since, as we have seen, the schools have for the most part already abandoned the serious study of literature. The same holds true for the preservation of history and philosophy and foreign languages. When these disciplines disappear from the college curriculum they disappear from American culture.

But even in the literature classrooms where the rapidly diminishing number of college students who do not elect to study literature much less to major in it, conditions are rarely good for preserving the best that has been thought and said in the world. One of the most recent and ominous developments which the NEH report also deplores is the politicization of the study of literature, that is, selecting literature texts for study not because they represent the wisdom and beauty of the ages but because they represent special social, political, and philosophical interests not reflected in the traditional canon. Among the other dangers which this trend presents is that it tends to emphasize modern and contemporary literature at the expense of literature which is patently superior in its aesthetic and moral powers, and hence in its powers for producing pleasure and therefore its potential for awakening in students a love for the best literature. Much of the literature which has thus found its way into college literature classes is intended to reflect the particular interests of Marxists, feminists, and minorities, and is chosen not because it is the greatest literature in the world but because it reaffirms what Marxists, feminists, and ethnic minorities want to reaffirm, regardless of how limited its universal aesthetic and moral appeal may be. Much of that literature was written in the twentieth century and is often literature written since 1950. To make way for this kind of literature something has to go, and what usually goes are the texts which represent the highest literary achievement of our civilization and even of the twentieth century itself. And since the professors individually choose the literature, they tend to choose what they want to teach rather than what they should teach and thus strike a further blow to the possibility of preserving a literary canon.

The press has called attention to the phenomenon of the traditional literary canon under siege in the universities. *The New York Times*, for example, observed (January 6, 1987) that an increasing number of university faculty "contend that the idea of an enduring pantheon of writers and their works is an elitist one largely defined by white men who are northeastern academics and critics, and who believe in the teaching of writers principally for their historical and sociological importance, for what they have to say rather than how well they say it." And Jonathan Yardly, columnist for *The Washington Post*, (January 14, 1988) observed that many professors are "busily at work on their own hidden agenda," which involves "institiutionalizing the political sentiments that were prevalent on the campuses two decades ago." And he concludes: "It is no exaggeration to say that literature itself is not an issue here at all, for these people simply do not understand or care about literature as the term traditionally has been understood. Not merely are they careerists and political schemers; they are also children of the age of semiotics and deconstruction, an age in which it is taught in the English departments that the critic is more important than the artist and that the interpretation is more important than the work." In some universities deconstruction has gone so far that students are asked to study only the criticism, chiefly the criticism which deconstructs literary works, including the literary masterpieces, without assigning the literary works themselves, leaving one to wonder how low the universities can go in destroying not only the canon of the best literature but the authority of literature itself.

The Marxist approach to literature is also well represented, in the larger universities especially, often under the aegis of influential Marxist critics, who play a major role in contemporary American criticism. The effect of their influence is to attempt to alter the literary canon to include the study of literature which reflects Marxist aims and which usually relies upon recent literary works to the neglect or rejection of, or worse, the misinterpretation of the best writers.

Similarly, the feminist movement in America makes itself felt in the literary curriculum by emphasizing or reinterpreting literary works which reflect their own interests, not necessarily the interests of women in general but of feminists in particular. One well-known feminist professor of literature wrote in *The Chronicle for Higher Education* (August 8, 1988) that "we were the first to act openly on the principle that the literary canon is, among other things, an instrument for legitimatizing not only aesthetic but also social and political values in our culture," specifically their own peculiar social and literary values.

In fact, the threat to the traditional literary canon in the colleges and universities is part of a larger controversy over the whole question of whether or not the teaching of Western thought ought to be abandoned in favor of a broader study of world cultures, particularly third-world and minority cultures. Increasingly the question is being raised as to whether or not emphasis should be shifted from our cultural heritage to everyone else's cultural heritage. Other interests also insist that more time and space should be given to popular culture, including the serious study of mystery, detective, and romance novels. This kind of thinking is being led by the cultural left, which wields enormous influence over the curriculum in many college and university English departments.

Those who advocate this kind of end-run around the traditional curriculum do not, of course, have everything their own way. A number of recent influential spokesmen for the preservation of the study of the great literature include the former Secretary of Education William J. Bennett, Allan Bloom, author of *The Closing of the American Mind*, E.D. Hirsch, author of *Cultural Literacy*, and Lynne V. Cheney, former chairman of the National Endowment for the Humanities, who in the work already cited came out strongly for the "truths that, transcending accidents of class, race, and gender, speak to us all." Even more attacks upon the liberal academic establishment include Jacques Barzun's *The Culture We Deserve*, Peter Shaw's *The War Against the Intellect*, Jeffrey Hart's *Acts of Recovery*, Page Smith's *Killing the Spirit*, and Wendell Harris's *Reclaiming the Study of Literature*. And there are others, both in book and article form, enough to call attention to the fact that all is not well in the teaching of the humanities in academe. National organizations have also been formed in an attempt to stanch the flood of principles and practices which are destroying the humanities in general and literature in particular. In addition there are also some universities and plenty of colleges which are not easily persuaded to venture far onto untried academic and anti-academic territory.

*****

This controversy is likely to rage for a long time to come, and at this juncture it is difficult to identify which movements are merely fads and which will represent the mainstream of intellectual history. The intellectual atmosphere in the universities tends to favor the eventual victory of those seeking variety in the college curriculum at the expense of the traditional curriculum because the academic establishment tends to be stacked with far more liberals than conservatives. At the very least, however, it may be said that there is little hope, at least in the near future, for help from our education system in preserving the great literary tradition of the Western world, for if our schools and colleges and graduate schools had deliberately set out to gradually destroy it they could hardly be more successful than they are now.

Chapter IV

Literature Versus the Electronic Age

One of the most persistent threats to a thriving literary tradition is the fact that for most people, watching and listening are more pleasurable than reading. They are also easier than reading, which in part explains why they are more pleasurable. Most people would rather hear a story or watch it acted out than read it. Even those who are highly literate and who read serious literature, oftentimes succumb to the pleasures of listening and watching in preference to reading. Those who are illiterate have no choice but to watch and listen and the semi-literature have a limited choice. Even before the advent of the audio-visual age, reading in general and reading serious literature in particular has always been the privilege of the few, but its prestige was high partly because there was no other way to tell stories except the limited accessibility of oral tradition and the theater. The advent of the electronic age, however, brought endless alternatives to reading novels, plays, and short fiction, and indeed to most forms of the written word.

Before discussing the nature of this threat, I should like to make some observations about the crucial importance of the written word to the humanities in general as well as to literature itself. Just as certain kinds of knowledge and experience can best, indeed only. come from seeing and hearing, so also certain kinds of knowledge and experience can come only, or at least best, from the written word. Indeed the highest orders of truth can come almost solely from the written word, namely the truths of philosophy, of history, and of literature. These kinds of truths are called the humanities because they are the result of the peculiarly human faculties, faculties which men possess, but which beasts do not possess, namely the faculties, respectively of reason, of memory, and of the imagination. The truths which the exercise of these faculties convey depend almost entirely upon the written word to properly convey them. The nature of literature, by its very etymological definition, is the written word; philosophy, which deals exclusively with concepts depends upon the written word because only words can effectively communicate philosophical concepts, and the study of historical periods before the advent of the audio-visual age depended entirely upon the written word. History even now depends mostly on the written word because even though audio-visual aids can contribute something to an understanding of history, it is poorly served without the written word since the continuity and grand sweep of history cannot be understood except through the written word. The truths of religion, which are the truths of God, also depend upon the authority of the written word because all the influential religions are based upon a body of sacred scripture which claims divine origin or sanction.

But the highest role and goal of literature, philosophy, and history— and religion—have been to search out the truths of moral man, to determine and to show men what the moral truths are and how and why they should guide human behavior. From the time of the ancient Greeks until the last century, the *moral* purpose of literature, of philosophy, and of history has been axiomatic on the grounds that there is no more effective way of perpetuating moral truths. And as we have seen, during the Renaissance they were all regarded as handmaidens of religion. Sir Philip Sidney was eager to demonstrate that literature, even more than philosophy and history, best leads to virtuous action. He saw with crystal clarity that science and mathematics can not, and the faculties of imagination, reason, and memory were the faculties that could. Nor can the behavioral sciences, since they too depend exclusively upon the peculiarly scientific method of counting and measuring, without the capacity of dealing with the truths of moral man. For example, the social sciences such as psychology, sociology and economics deal only with how moral man acts, not with how he ought to act, without borrowing the methods of the humanities.

Such, then, is the everlasting role of the humanities, a role that no other disciplines can provide. In an age where the authority of religion is increasingly losing out, particularly among intellectuals, the humanities are the only ways left to us in our attempt to deal with the great questions of how people *ought* to act. Except for the truths of religion, they are, then, concerned exclusively with the most durable kinds of truths, and they should thus be cherished by the most highly developed civilizations. But the humanities depend for their survival upon the continued prestige of the printed page. The corollary is that as the prestige of the printed page falls, so falls the prestige of the humanities.

If the humanities are to be preserved, what must also be preserved is what might be called a "print-oriented" tradition. By a print-oriented person I mean one who habitually *prefers* the authority of the printed word to the authority of sights and sounds. This is not to say that sights and sounds are not the best authority in the perpetuation of important kinds of truths. For some kinds of truths, for example, scientific truths, they are the only authority. But there are many times when one has the choice of either written sources or audio-visual sources. It is in these instances when the truly print-oriented person prefers written sources. He would prefer, for example, to get the news from newspapers or news magazines rather then from television; he would prefer to read history from books rather than from audio-visual documentaries, especially since such sources can deal with history only in fragments and usually only recent history; he would prefer to study philosophical truths in the form of the printed page rather than through oral tradition; and he would prefer the emotional experiences which novels and stories can provide to what motion pictures can provide. Yet the print-oriented person is becoming an endangered species, and partially as a result so too are the humanities in general and our literary tradition in particular.

The chief point I wish to make in this chapter is that the twentieth century audio-visual revolution is one more major threat to the preservation of our literary heritage because it is a major threat to a print-oriented society. It is a threat which comes both from inside the school walls and outside the school walls. It would appear, in fact, that the threat from inside the schools is even greater than from outside the schools.

Print-oriented people can be produced only by our educational system because that is where they learn to read, and therefore can become print-oriented. And yet our education system is failing badly in turning out print-oriented students not only because of the unworkable methods of teaching students to read as described in the previous chapter, but also because the audio-visual revolution has invaded the schools as thoroughly as it has invaded adult life. The schools in fact dramatize perhaps more effectively than any other part of society how thoroughly both looking and listening have succeeded in replacing reading and writing. The written word has now to compete intensely against "audio-visual aids," which have come to permeate classes from the first grade through the twelfth.

Schools begin, in fact, with the "basal" readers in the first grade. They are almost a symbol of the force of the audio-visual revolution, for these readers are illustrated so lavishly that the first words which appear on these pages seem almost as if they were being pushed off. A sample page of a first-grade reader might show an illustration of a purple hippopotamus so huge that the half dozen or so words which appear on the page are huddled together as if in self-defense. It has commonly been regarded as a great pedagogical triumph that modern elementary school readers have huge illustrations on every page, as if somehow floods of colorful pictures enhance the student's ability and desire to read. In fact, some reader series suggest that students should try to guess the meaning of the words by looking at the pictures.

These illustrations continue in vast numbers and in vast sizes not only thorough the elementary grades but through the middle grades as well, though by then the are usually smaller and less frequent. Even the high school literature books sport lavish illustrations. It can probably be far better argued that the profusion of pictures distracts students and even retards the learning process than that it helps it. By comparison, the fifth-grade McGuffey reader, from the series already alluded to, has only 14 illustrations in its 360 pages of rich literature, and some of the illustrations look as though they are about to be pushed off the page by the large quantities of normal-sized print. Illustrations in reader series in European schools are generally also used sparingly on the grounds that they interfere with the business of teaching students to read.

It should be said at the outset that the judicious use of audio-visual aids in the classroom can be educationally advantageous, and it would be folly not to make use of them since they exist and since in certain ways and in certain intellectual areas there is no substitute for them. Socrates himself would have used them if he could. But what ought to be recognized is that audio-visual aids are now revolutionizing the educational process in American schools to the point that they constitute a serious threat to the authority of the written word at all grade levels, and are even making dangerous inroads in the colleges.

How far audio-visual techniques have penetrated the schools is suggested by the fact that they have led to the introduction of a whole new vocabulary into the educational process. School libraries, for example, are no longer called libraries but "media centers" or sometimes "learning resource centers," in order to accommodate the new emphasis upon non-print pedagogical methods. The printed word has become only one of the "multi-media" and not necessarily the most important. There is even something called "visual literacy" and another called "aural literacy," as well as "computer literacy,"—all contradictions in terms in view of the root meaning of *literacy*.

All of these concepts reflect the fact that audio-visual aids are not merely a minor adjunct to the learning process but are on their way to taking over the learning process, so that print media in some schools become mere aids to audio-visual learning. "Educational media" and "educational technology" are now the order of the day. They have not so much to do with the written word as with television sets, record players, film strips, video tapes, audio cassettes, teaching machines, motion pictures, and above all, computers.

Computers are in fact about to overwhelm all the other audio-visual pedagogical aids. The aim in many if not most schools is to have a computer terminal for every student in the school, and the only reason keeping some schools from doing so is the lack of money to purchase them. There is much, however, to be said for computers as a teaching tool. Perhaps the point to be made here about computers in the schools is that they can be wondrous helps for students in reading, in geography, in the sciences, in mathematics, and in foreign languages, as well as other areas of learning. They may in fact provide a strong incentive for students to learn to read since most serious use of computers involves the written word, even if not the printed page.

They cannot, however, be used successfully in the teaching of either history or literature. These are what might be called hard-core print disciplines, because, as we have seen, they depend almost wholly on the written word for their mastery. And since it is not likely that many students will be willing to read large amounts of literary or history texts on their computers, the book is the best alternative, indeed the only really practical alternative. The computer can play no important role in the preservation of a student's literary heritage, but the computer has become so idolized as a teaching tool that there is always the possible danger that in the future if literature cannot be taught on the computer it will not be taught at all.

Needless to say, there are plenty of pedagogical hardware businesses around to see that the schools are well-stocked with every kind of audio-visual equipment, on the grounds that there is no educational job that audio-visual aids can't do or help do. Audio-visual aids for schools already constitute an enterprise running into the billions of dollars, and even draw the financial support of the federal government.

The pleasures of reading are often no match for the pleasures of manipulating electronic contraptions from the first grade through the twelfth, especially in the experience of millions of students who are not at home with the printed page. Furthermore, teachers and students and administrators who don't have teaching machines, film strips, slide projectors, tapes, cassettes, record players and computers look with longing and envy on those who do because they tend to believe that these devices provide more learning, and certainly more fun. In fact, one of the attractions of audio-visual devices is that they conform to one of the most fundamental premises of modern American pedagogy, namely that learning should above all be fun; that it should not only be free from pain but full of pleasure, and that if it is painful it should be avoided. However popular this premise is, it directly contradicts the observation of Aristotle, who in his wisdom perceived that "all learning is accompanied by pain," and its corollary that where there is no pain there is no learning.

A classic example of the way in which electronic media have contributed to driving the written word out of the classroom is the advent of the language laboratory in the teaching of foreign languages in the schools (and colleges). The language laboratory became popular in response to a new approach to the teaching of foreign language which developed in the 1950s and which came to be known as the "oral-aural approach" or the "audio-lingual approach."

This method insists that the best way to learn a foreign language is first to learn to speak it and understand it, and then, if there happen to be any years left over, to learn to read and write it. The language laboratory, it was widely thought, would do much to help the student learn to speak a foreign language. It enabled him to listen to his own bad pronunciation with the hope that he might correct it, and it gave him listening practice so that he could perhaps come to understand a few spoken words as well. A multitude of languages could be piped simultaneously into a multitude of student ears through headphones in private booths with a single teacher or assistant at the console controls. The federal government became so excited about the possibilities that it donated hundreds of millions of dollars to schools and colleges throughout the country for language laboratories. In fact, the foreign language laboratory has become the very core of the foreign language program in most American schools and colleges.

In time, however, the wiser sort of foreign language instructors recognized that at the end of a year or two years of this kind of instruction most students still could neither speak nor understand their foreign language very well. Anyone who doubts the sorry results of this newer way of teaching foreign languages need only speak a little German or Spanish or French or Russian with a student a year or two after he has finished the course in order to see for himself how close the effort comes to being a total waste. Meanwhile, the emphasis upon reading and writing has been to a remarkable degree neglected. The typical student who has tried to learn a language by the oral-aural approach and the language laboratory cannot get past the first sentence of a foreign language newspaper much less write a decent letter in the language. Thus in the end, unless the student studies a language for three or preferably four or five years, he ends up not being able to speak, understand, read, or write the language he has been studying. Nonetheless, this method overwhelmingly dominates foreign language instruction today both in the schools and the colleges so that the literary value of the foreign language remains unknown to virtually all high school graduates and to most college graduates. Americans thus deserve their notorious reputation for not knowing foreign languages.

But other pedagogical practices have also been at work to quash the value of the written word in the classroom besides the abuse of audio-visual and electronic equipment. Students today, especially in elementary schools and even middle schools, engage in a wide variety of other activities in the classroom that have little or nothing to do with the written word, activities ranging from putting on skits and puppet shows to making posters, models, and displays.

If elementary school students study a unit on American Indians, for example, they may make Indian costumes, perform Indian dances, make Indian wampum and Indian pottery, hold an Indian pow-wow, visit an Indian village, see a movie about Indians, hear some Indian songs, and if there is any time left over, they may even read a little bit about Indians. An article in a professional journal describes a fairly typical non-reading middle-school program of world culture, in which students "paint, dance, exercise, cook, build, create, write, sing, listen and enjoy themselves"; i.e., they do everything but read about the countries they are studying.

Other symptoms of the ascendancy of the anti-print revolution in the schools include the dramatic decline in writing requirements and the reluctance to give meaningful homework assignments, particularly those which require reading or writing. Everyone from professors of education down through school administrators, teachers, and even the students themselves, and often their parents, know that writing has been all but phased out of the school curriculum. Some schools, it is true, give more attention to writing than others. In fact, in some school systems students may even do a great deal of writing in the way of reports, themes, research papers and perhaps even stories and poems. But even in these schools the writing experience is rarely sustained, and the writing efforts of students oftentimes are not carefully corrected or criticized.

The widespread practice of abandoning or reducing homework assignments in many schools reflects the letting up of the emphasis upon the written word. This practice has behind it the same philosophy of educational permissiveness and anti-intellecualism that has inspired many other pedagogical innovations which allow students to avoid using their minds in any rigorous way, including especially broad and truly challenging experiences with the written word.

There is a book entitled *The Audio-Visual Man*, which dreams of a future in which the written word will have virtually disappeared from civilization and in which men communicate among themselves solely through non-conceptual media, i. e., through sights and sounds. It points out with some enthusiasm how far Western civilization has already moved in that direction by observing that "Yesterday, there were textbooks and blackboards; today, television and computer teaching. Yesterday, communications by letter and public speaking; today tape recorders, telephones, records and films."

The ultimate audio-visual man, one may suppose, is also illiterate man, a person living in a civilization where there is no longer any need for the printed word. There seems to be plenty of evidence that American schools are well on their way to turning out a new product, namely the audio-visual student, the student who communicates exclusively by sights and sounds.

But the world is not yet ready for the audio-visual student. Some degree of genuine literacy is still required in almost all occupations which promise or indeed don't promise a future. Most high school dropouts are audio-visual persons because reading is so badly taught in many schools, and they in general face a bleak future. A fairly high degree of literacy is also required for successful college work, which helps explain why so many students, approximately half, who enter college do not finish.

The authority of the written word is not entirely safe, however, even in higher education, for the audio-visual revolution has reached the college classrooms too in the form of television, video tapes, motion pictures, and above all the non-print use of computers. The communications major, for example, has become extraordinarily popular in recent decades, and flocks of students are now rushing to major in it—in approximate proportions to the drop in English majors—because there appears to be a growing market for communications graduates. Yet it deals largely in non-print forms of communication, namely sights and sounds, and as a result some communications majors also come close to being audio-visual students. Manufacturers of audio-visual equipment are at work now quite as diligently in the colleges selling their hardware and software, and with increasing success, even in humanities courses. In fact, textbook publishers at both the college level and the school level are more and more offering lines of motion pictures and video casettes of novels, usually, to be sure, with accompanying "workbooks"; but nevertheless publishers of textbooks perceive the certain and rapid shift away from books to motion pictures and television and computer screens in the classroom, and this revolution is merely in its infancy. Again, partly as a result of these new trends, many college graduates are coming closer and closer to being audio-visual students.

It will be obvious enough that all this new emphasis upon the sights and sounds of learning does not bode well for the future of the written word in general or the future of literature in particular. If the perpetuation of our literary tradition depends upon a print-oriented society, then the schools are increasingly failing to provide it. The schools tend to reinforce the idea that learning through listening and watching is not only an easier way of learning but a superior way of learning, and there is almost the assumption that if it can't be seen or heard it isn't worth learning. But the literary experience is not a listening or watching experience; it is not a perceptual experience but a conceptual experience. The pleasure and profit do not come primarily from the sound of the words even in poetry, or the design of the letters or words on the printed page. It comes from the conceptualizing of words and sentences and paragraphs and stories or chapters which the mind is capable of fashioning without any pleasurable appeal of what is seen or heard. And even though print-oriented people know this kind of experience to be superior, and indeed more pleasurable than any kind of learning that the senses can offer, the schools are producing fewer and fewer print-oriented students because they do so much to encourage non-print experiences in the classroom.

*****

But the decline of a print-oriented society is the result not only of the increasing role of audio-visual media among students but among adults as well. The flood of electronic media in the world at large is rapidly turning adults as well as students into audio-visual addicts, more interested in what they watch than what they read. Television tends to kill the literary instinct in its viewers, so that even highly literate adults are mesmerized by the images they see and the sounds that they hear on the screen. Television has become the Siren song of popular culture and very few can avoid it. It wields the power to destroy interest in the written word for those whose interest was already tenuous, and it can at least dent the interest of those who cherish the written word, including those who have experienced the advanced pleasures and profit of the best fiction and poetry. When couch potatoes curl up in front of a fire, it is rarely to read a good novel, or even a bad novel, but to watch television. The last reported record holder of continued television watching is a 24-year-old Australian carpenter, who watched his television screen continuously for 168 hours, and insisted at the end of the experience that he still loved television (*Newsweek*, October 27, 1988,p. 93). Our capacities for watching television have not even come close to being tapped. Neither, of course, have our capacities for using computers, though computers have the undisputed advantage over television of communicating by means of the written word, at least much of the time, though computer games are there for the taking for both children and adults, and they are taking them in increasing numbers.

Similarly the advent of VCR's now owned by the majority of households in America have also captured a large portion of the idle time of Americans. At some public libraries patrons check out more video cassettes than they do books, to the point that libraries are complaining that they can't supply them fast enough to satisfy the demand. The public library is thus a kind of echo of what is going on in the homes and in the schools, and it seems to underline a kind of inevitability that the world of the printed word is being replaced at a dizzying pace by the audio-visual world.

No one should be deluded into believing that watching a novel dramatized on television is the equivalent experience or even a superior experience, to reading it. The audio-visual experience dulls the imagination, saturates the senses, diminishes the pleasures of the intellectual engagement, and is therefore far inferior to the literary experience. It is unlikely that any script for dramatizing a novel will approach the stature of serious literature, any more than an opera libretto can ever claim any great artistic achievement. A novelist is capable of portraying subtleties of action and character accompanied by the subtleties of emotional response in the reader which no motion picture of novel can hope to reproduce, and these subtleties are the source of vastly more pleasurable and rewarding effects for those equipped to experience them than any audio-visual experience can possibly be. Print-oriented audiences are quite aware of this fact, just as non-print oriented audiences cannot be made aware of it. It should be recognized, however, that there is not the same problem when plays with substantial literary merit are dramatized on the screen, for the best have genuine literary value, so that fidelity to the play itself not only provides the kind of pleasure proper to serious literature but heightened pleasure resulting from watching the performance.

But if an account of the present threat of the audio-visual revolution which has already taken place is not enough to discourage the print-oriented and particularly the literary-oriented segment of society, predictions of how much more formidable that threat will become in the next decade or two might lead with some justification to the conclusion that the printed page in general and literature in particular is on its last legs. For it is not difficult to imagine that further technological breakthroughs involving, for example, satellite transmission, the marriage of television and computers, the miracle of fibre optics, advanced cable systems, improved on-line technology and other probable developments which will hasten the maturing of the electronic age will profoundly affect how the audio-visual revolution will influence all our lives.

Thus, the number of ways in which the revolution in communications is displacing and will increasingly continue to displace the written page can boggle the mind. This new emphasis upon communicating by sights and sounds even by itself puts the future of literature in serious jeopardy. It is actually a far greater potential threat than any of the others I have identified in this study. One of the reasons is that there does not seem to be any stopping further development of electronic wonders which entice both students and adults away from the artistic forms of the written word, whereas philosophies and pedagogical techniques, including better methods of teaching reading, can be changed and hence dramatically improve the prospects for the future of literature, so that a rediscovery of the importance of literature to individuals and societies and indeed civilizations is theoretically possible were it not for the triumph of electronic communications.

Meanwhile, what is crucial to remember is that the systematic study of the humanities—philosophy, history, and literature—depend for their very existence upon the book, not the screen, and when the book goes then the humanities, including literature, go with it. And is it too much to say that civilization also goes with it?

Chapter V

The Power of Literature

The foregoing chapters of this study have suggested something of the variety and strength of the forces which have trivialized literature in recent decades; and yet literature remains not only a powerful means of communicating with words the essential nature of the human condition but even a way of improving it. The literary imagination enjoys the unique combination of appealing simultaneously to the intellect and to the emotions through the medium of words. Philosophy does not qualify, nor does history, nor do the pure sciences or mathematics, or the behavioral sciences nor indeed any other discipline which depends exclusively upon human faculties.

Among all these kinds of learning, literature does not have its equal. "No learning is so good as that which teacheth and moveth to virtue," said Sir Philip Sidney, "and that none can both teach and move thereto so much as poetry [i.e., all imaginative literature], then is the conclusion manifest that ink and paper cannot be to more profitable purpose employed." I do not claim more for literature than Sidney claimed for it; but I do claim that the literary experience can produce a more powerful moral-aesthetic effect upon the reader that many other kinds of vicarious experience can provide. Indeed the heart of my argument is that it is the peculiar combination of the moral and aesthetic experience, through the use of words, that gives literature its unique power.

I should like to begin with this assertion of the power of literature by raising the most basic of all the questions about literature, namely, What is or ought to be its purpose, its *raison d'être*, its final cause? That is the question which needs most urgently to be answered; and yet, as I have suggested, it is the very question which literary theorists in the twentieth century have been most reluctant to face.

The mainstream twentieth century literary theories described in Chapter II of this study tend either to ignore entirely the question of the purpose of literature or else to offer answers which in one way or another trivialize it. The expressionistic theory defines the purpose of literature in terms of its effect upon the author rather than upon the audience, and therefore leads quite logically to obscurantism and formlessness, as some contemporary literature illustrates, and in its extreme manifestation, particularly in lyric poetry, downright unintelligibility. The hedonistic theory trivializes literature by denying the moral purpose of literature, and hence regards it as merely one more source of pleasure not basically unlike any other. As we have seen too from Chapter II of this study, historical critics, biographical critics, the New Critics, the structuralists critics and myth critics and psychological critics, and other critical schools which offer mere fact-finding approaches to the study of literature, do not even entertain the question of the ultimate purpose of literature. They are not really critics at all, but elucidators, exegetes, and professional analyzors, with no full-fledged apparatus to demonstrate that literature is anything like the highest form of earthly learning. Nor do most of them even have a workable method of determining whether one literary work is better or worse than any other. The Marxist and feminist critics, and others of the multitudes of critical schools which politicize literature, even though they have well-defined views of the purpose of literature, represent special interest groups, so that they tend to denigrate great works of literature which will not pass their tests, and to elevate undeserving works that do.

Is there, then, a theory of literature which avoids the pitfalls of modern critical theorists and which can reassert the primacy of literature over the other humanistic disciplines? I think that there is, and the aim of this chapter is to propose it.

Perhaps there is no better place to begin a general discussion of the purpose of literature than with the Horatian formula, which holds that the aim of literature is "to teach and to delight." The phrase has been cited time and again by critics from the Middle Ages and

Renaissance until the nineteenth century as a short and convenient way of answering this most crucial of literary questions of literary theory. Neither Horace nor most of those who quoted Horace felt bound to explain precisely *how* literature pleases, and *how* it instructs. But it was a lucky phrase, a convenient tag, as many of the quotations in the Appendix of this study will suggest. At the same time it is also an extremely important concept, because that is what literature actually does do, or should do.

Two persistent theories of the purpose of literature have prevailed almost from the beginning of the history of literary criticism: namely the didactic theory and the hedonistic theory. William Wimsatt and Cleanth Brooks in their *Literary Criticism: A Short History* point out that even Hellenistic criticism argued over these two theories. I quote:

> The question [was] whether the function of poetry is hedonistic or didactic—whether the correct view is the Ionian and Homeric, that the aim of poetry is pleasure through enchantment, or the Boetian and Hesiodic, that it is teaching. Stoic philosophers held more or less consistently to the contentual or didactic view. Professional scholars and critics, like Heracliodorus and Eratosthenes, dwelt on diversion and the enchantment of beautiful words.

But the hedonistic theory of literature did not thrive in the classical world as much as it is sometimes made out to have done. Something more was always demanded of literature than mere delight. It had somehow to "improve" the audience. At the same time there was no denying that literature is a source of delight, and so the combination of "teaching" and "delighting," as Horace would have it, informed virtually all literary theory until a hundred or so years ago, by which time, as we have seen, literary critics began to disengage literature from morality.

What seemed to be left, then, was the didactic theory. Literary critics from the Middle Ages on through the Renaissance and even through the eighteenth century tended to subscribe to the didactic theory because that was the theory which most clearly demonstrated that literature had a serious moral purpose, and medieval and Renaissance literature was flooded with didactic works as a way of protecting literature against the charge of frivolousness or immorality.

But the didactic theory of literature, despite its dominant popularity in the Middle Ages and the Renaissance, is beset by serious difficulties.

Edgar Allan Poe rightfully called this theory a "heresy." What is there about the didactic theory of literature which makes it a heresy? Perhaps the best definition of didactic literature is that it is literature in which the author is more interested in the general than in the particular. The didactic theory presumes that the purpose of literature is to couch some moral or philosophical truth in the delights of a story. It assumes that the author uses the particulars of a story as merely a device to enforce a general "lesson." One of the major difficulties, then, about didactic literature is that it is regularly open to the charge of artistic insincerity in the sense that the author is not sharing or trying to understand his characters' emotions or to get worked up by them, and that therefore the reader does not see why he himself should get excited either. A ready example would be an Aesop fable, say, the story of "The Tortoise and the Hare." It is clear that what Aesop is primarily interested in doing is teaching the reader about the advantages of being slow and steady over the danger of being overconfident. He is not excited about tortoises or hares; he merely *uses* tortoises and hares to make his point. Similarly, in a more sophisticated, indeed spectacular exercise in didacticism, Spenser, in *The Faerie Queene*, is more interested in communicating the value and importance of holiness than he is in presenting Red Cross Knight as a character to be taken seriously. He may hope, of course, that the reader will accept Red Cross Knight as much a genuine character as any other character—and to a remarkable degree he succeeds—but there is no getting around the fact that he merely stands for something, namely Holiness.

The allegorical method is characteristically didactic because it is evident that the allegorist is more interested in the general than the particular. He doesn't offer up his characters as believable human beings but as abstractions representing certain human characteristics. The author knows it and the reader knows it. The novelist, on the other hand, finds the audience more willing to accept his characters because he does not *use* them but offers them sincerely as believable people.

But didactic literature does not have to be allegorical to be didactic. Any story in which the characters merely serve to illustrate general principles is to some degree didactic, as I have defined the term. There are, of course, infinite degrees of didacticism. In some works the didacticism is heavy-handed, and in other works it my be so subtle as to be almost imperceptible.

Many works of the Medieval and Renaissance periods and even later, for example, preserved the story-teller's art up until the very end, but then concluded with a "moral," a practice which perhaps may do little to weaken the artistry of the work but which suggests the tenacity of the didactic tradition. But many plays or narratives, from the Middle Ages on through the eighteenth century and beyond, are heavily didactic. In these, it is as if the author were trying to hoodwink the reader, which is why the didactic theory is sometimes called the sugar-coated pill theory. As Keats once observed, "We hate poetry that has a palpable design on us."

But there is another problem with the didactic method, namely that most of the great literature of the world (and most of the not so great too) is not didactic, so that it becomes difficult to advocate a literary theory which most of the literature of the world violates. Almost all of the great works of literature from the early Greeks on through the twentieth century, whether by Homer, Virgil, Shakespeare, Milton, Dickens, Dostoevsky, Tolstoy, or hundreds of the other great novelists and dramatists and epic and narrative and lyric poets are not didactic. It is difficult to find a "moral" in them such as can readily be found in an Aesop fable. The didactic method, for all its moral earnestness, is thus not the way to reclaim literature as the highest form of earthly learning.

But neither, as we have seen, is the hedonistic theory. Poe, in observing that the didactic theory is a "heresy" proceeded to propose the only other theory he knew, namely the hedonistic theory. Like his French disciples, including Baudelaire, and American and British advocates of the hedonistic school of literature, Poe did not perceive it to be a heresy, even though, as we have seen, the rise of the hedonistic theory of literature has done much to trivialize literature because it demeans it.

The didactic theory and the hedonistic theory represent something like the Scylla and Charibdis of literary criticism. Both tend to destroy the efficacy of literature, and it is difficult to steer a middle course. Horace seemed to do so, and hence the popularity of the Horatian formula, though neither he nor his disciples seem ever to have plotted a safe route between them. Teachers frequently teach students in school to look for a moral in a literary work and when they don't find one, as for example, in a Shakespeare play, they, like their teachers, are often puzzled and may find it difficult to determine wherein the moral value of the work lies, or to conclude that it doesn't have any. Sometimes this kind of problem can appear in college classes as well, so that there is often a continual bouncing between the whirlpool and the monster.

The problem remains, then, to develop a theory of literature which avoids the deadly pitfalls of both the trivializing effect of the hedonistic theory and the suffocating effect of the didactic theory, as well as recourse to the mere political or social value of a literary work. What is required is a theory which reaffirms both the delight and the moral force of literature and a universal value to literature and which is applicable to virtually all literary works in a way that these theories are not, a theory which can honestly claim literature to be the highest form of earthly learning.

Such a theory must first of all maintain that the ultimate purpose of literature is the moral effect upon the reader. However unpopular, even outmoded, this fundamental premise may seem in the twentieth century, it has two arguments in favor of it: first, it is the theory based upon a perception of human nature which, as we have seen, dominated the history of literary criticism from the fourth century B. C. until well into the nineteenth century, namely that human nature is imperfect and that literature can improve it. Second, it is the only theory which can make the claims for literature which Sir Philip Sidney and John Dennis and Samuel Johnson and Percy Bysshe Shelley and Matthew Arnold and the other great defenders of literature have made for it.

It should be recognized too that there have been literary critics and theorists in the twentieth century who have held out for the principle of the moral value of literature. They include Paul Elmer More in *The Shelburne Lectures,* Irving Babbitt in *Rousseau and Romanticism*, Yvor Winters in *In Defense of Reason,* F. R. Leavis in *The Great Tradition*, Randall Stewart in *American Literature and Christian Doctrine,* David Noble in *The American Adam and the New Word Garden*, and John Gardner in *The Idea of Moral Criticism*, among others. All in varying ways and with varying degrees of zeal argue for the moral purpose of literature, but those who are the most insistent in their arguments, such as More, Babbitt, and Winters, tend to be regarded as outsiders, if not pariahs.

The chief reason that the idea of the moral purpose of literature is unpopular is that most literary critics today do not really believe in the moral purpose of literature. As a result, the vast majority of literary critics—and undoubtedly many professors and teachers of literature as well—do not themselves believe that literature is the highest form of earthly learning, or anywhere near it. Or at the very least they do not see how it can be. Some are so far under the influence of the scientific spirit that they concentrate on the "facts" of a literary work and ignore its real power, which lies in the emotional effect upon an audience experiencing the literary representations of human actions. Others tend to be so far under the influence of the hedonistic theory, which has been building since the early nineteenth century, that "the moral purpose of literature" has become a dirty phrase, even though in literary theory from the time of the ancient Greeks through most of the 18h century it was a universal premise. Still others among the burgeoning group of critics insist that the true end of literature is, as we have seen, to advance any of a number of political causes.

Another reason that the theory of the moral purpose of literature is unpopular is that such a theory immediately become associated with the didactic theory, as I have suggested in the brief discussion of the controversy between John Crowe Ransom and Yvor Winters over the purpose of literature. It is by no means clear even to many *literateurs* how literature can be moral without having a moral. In fact, some of the most trenchant attacks upon literature which is perceived as being didactic have come from those who, like Ransom, subscribe, however tacitly, to the hedonistic view of the purpose of literature. Thus, one of the major difficulties in developing a theory which insists upon the moral purpose of literature is to make clear how literature can be moral without having a moral.

*****

The first principle in developing such a theory is to recognize a fundamental psychological phenomenon concerning the emotional reaction of the reader to a novel or story, or, in the case of an audience, to a play (or to a motion picture, for that matter). For reasons which probably no one fully understands, the reader of a novel or the spectator at a play is capable of the sensation of actually being the character portrayed in the novel or on the stage or screen, especially the main character, and at the same time of being aware that he or she is not the character but is merely observing the character's actions. In other words, there is something in the human make-up which permits the reader or the spectator to experience simultaneously both empathy and sympathy for the characters, both identification and non-identification.

This phenomenon of identification and non-identification may be illustrated thus: Suppose that a spectator is watching a television movie in which a hunter in the wilds of Africa comes across a lion and that the lion, seeing the hunter, charges him. Let us suppose that the hunter raises his rifle and aims it at the lion but that the rifle misfires. It appears that something in the psychological make-up of the spectator permits him to identify himself with the hunter and hence to experience the emotion of fear, not to say terror. But the spectator knows too that he is not the hunter and that he is comfortably seated on the sofa eating popcorn and is merely watching the hunter as he is about to be chewed to pieces by the lion. The emotional response from the non-identification phenomenon, then, is pity, so that the spectator experiences simultaneously both pity and terror.

There appears to be, then, a simultaneous sensation of empathy and sympathy. This phenomenon, however simplified in this example, provides a basis for a theory of literature which can insist upon both the aesthetic and the moral power of literature, and at the same time provide the basis for claiming that literature is the highest form of earthly learning.

I should like first to discuss in some detail the process of non-identification with the characters since it constitutes the heart of the moral force of the narrative in whatever form. Where non-identification is present, there are two possible emotions: sympathy or antipathy. Apathy is of course a third possibility, and results either from bad story-telling or imperceptive reading or viewing. Apathy (which in Greek means "without feeling") is the greatest enemy of the story-teller, for it causes the reader to close the novel he has been reading or to shut off the television set he has been watching. But there is no need to discuss it here. The point to be made about sympathy and antipathy is that they are *judicial* emotions; they imply approval or disapproval of what the characters are doing or what is being done to them. They are thus *moral* emotions, and they communicate moral judgments. Furthermore, in virtually all stories either one or both of these emotions are inevitable, almost no matter how hard the story-teller may try to avoid them. Even naturalistic writers like Gustave Flaubert or Emile Zola or Theodore Dreiser, however much they aim at a scientific detachment from their characters, cannot help making them sympathetic or unsympathetic.

What the story-teller does essentially is to represent his characters performing actions or a series of actions which make up the plot of the story, and, however consciously or unconsciously, to judge them by arousing the judicial emotions of sympathy or antipathy. By "action" I mean what Aristotle means, namely a decision or choice which demonstrates moral intent. No effective story-teller can escape from stories in which the characters demonstrate moral intent. It is on the basis of how characters habitually act and how they act in the story that the serious author conveys the unavoidable emotions of sympathy or antipathy.

In fact, one may inquire whether there has ever been a story in which the author did not portray any action which revealed moral intent and hence in which the emotions of sympathy or antipathy are not possible. There is at least one, and I should like to describe it here in order to illustrate the principle I am speaking of. The story is called *The Lady or the Tiger?* by Frank Stockton, once commonly anthologized in high school literature textbooks. The plot goes something like this: a princess is in love with a young man, who in turn is in love with a girl in the princess's train. The princess's father, in order to settle the problem, proposes that the young man be put in an arena with two doors, behind one of which is a tiger and behind the other of which is the girl he truly loves. It has been arranged beforehand that the princess, who knows who or what is behind each door, will sit in the box and is to signal to the young man which door he ought to open. The question then becomes: Is the princess so jealous of the girl that she signals to the young man to open the door behind which is the tiger, who will then come out and eat him up? Or is she so magnanimous in her love for him that she will signal to him to open the door behind which is the girl he loves and would thus get? How does the story end? Right there, and hence the title. The reader is left hanging, and as a result has no idea whether he ought to hate or admire her or whether the young man will find bliss in the end or death. *The Lady or the Tiger?* is a perfect example of a non-story. No moral choice is made, and hence the emotions of sympathy or antipathy are not possible. Furthermore, the reader's emotional involvement in the story is thus impossible, or else meaningless, and so the potential literary power of the story is wholly lost.

*****

But are there also stories in which the author describes a human experience but does not judge it? There would appear to be a good many of them, chief among which perhaps is the typical detective story. The purpose of the detective story is not to judge the murderer but simply to find out who the murderer is. It is true that a conventional ethic attaches to detective stories because, tacitly at least, the author does not approve of murder; but so far as the reader is concerned—and the author too—the main thing is not whether the murderer was morally wrong but rather who the murderer is. It is not an evaluation of what is done but simply a matter of who done it. Thus, reading a typical detective story is not primarily a moral experience or an emotional experience but an intellectual experience, and so the genre falls more or less into the category of an exercise in high-class puzzle solving. As such it does not generally place high in the hierarchy of literary genres.

But even more sophisticated literary efforts can be open to the charge of lacking moral earnestness, even when a moral action is described. Certain stories by Edgar Allan Poe, for example, despite the originality and artistic excellence of them, seem to be lacking in moral seriousness. An example might be *The Casque of Amontillado*, in which Poe seems to be willing to sacrifice or even abrogate any serious moral concern for the wrongness of the murder in order to concentrate on its cleverness. It is a story about Montressor, who, for reasons unknown, seeks revenge on a longtime enemy. His revenge is planned around the fact that he knows that his enemy has a weakness for fine wines. He thereupon invites him down into his wine cellar, and plies him with samples of his wine as they move along the spooky corridor. We are told mysteriously that Montressor has a trowel hidden beneath his cloak. When they reach the end of the cellar, where the best wine is kept, Montressor sets his victim down in a little room with a bottle of Amontillado and proceeds with brick and mortar, which had earlier been planted there, to brick up the fourth wall of the cell. His enemy, being so far gone in fine wine that he doesn't know what is happening, suddenly finds himself in total darkness and finally comes to the realize that he has been entombed alive. Montressor, meanwhile, coolly cleans off his trowel, and the story ends with the words: *Requiescat in pace* (May he rest in peace).

Now there is no doubt that a moral choice has been described here: Montressor killed a man in the most deliberate and awful fashion. But the question is, What is Poe's attitude toward Montressor? Does he look upon him as a villain and try to make the reader feel that Montressor ought not to kill men in that way or perhaps in any other way? Or is he so intrigued by the shrewd, indeed fiendish manner of the murder that he rather hopes that the reader will be more taken with the manner than the morality of it? In a sense, it would seem that Poe is no more concerned with the morality of the murder than the typical detective story writer. In fact, he may have the reader all agog that such ingenious methods can be used to kill a man.

There are stories, on the other hand, which make a clear-cut distinction between heroes and villains. In these stories the sympathy and antipathy which the story-teller intended to evoke are unmistakable, and there is at least an appearance of moral sincerity. Typical nineteenth century melodramas with the hapless heroine, the utter villain and the daring hero at least illustrate the fundamental conflict between good and evil; and the emotions of sympathy and antipathy, however crude, are inescapable. The typical Hollywood Western also fits the formula of characters easily identifiable as good or evil and hence in a raw, but often sincere manner, evoke strong emotions of sympathy for, say, Roy Rogers, and antipathy for the cattle rustlers. As a result of evoking these judgmental emotions, it may be said that the typical Western is generally a higher literary genre than the typical detective story because the detective story does not, by its very nature, seriously attempt to evoke judicial emotions.

But the chief problem with these typical good-versus-evil stories is that the formula for them is often all too conventional and too obvious. They tend to pall because the sympathy-antipathy experience is so crude that its emotional effect may even result in bathos. It must be said, however, that artistic perceptions among many readers and viewers, especially children, are so underdeveloped that the hero-villain kind of story is the only kind that they can emotionally respond to.

Sophisticated story-telling seems to require that the major character or characters have both faults and virtues, because they more nearly approach the conditions of real life. As Dostoevsky observed, "Man is a marvelous mingling of good and evil." In such stories the author presents complex characters who perform complex actions, and he is thus faced with a greater challenge of evoking the right degree of sympathy or antipathy toward them. In such stories there may be both wicked characters and virtuous characters, but the most interesting characters, usually including the main character, if there is one, are likely to be a complex of both good and bad motives, of moral weaknesses and strengths, of changes in moral intent and behavior. In fact, it is only with these kinds of characters that a truly serious if not great literary work can be achieved.

Shakespeare's *Othello* may serve as an example of how a story produces a moral effect without having a moral. I might preface this explanation with a passage from Boswell's *Life of Samuel Johnson*, in which Boswell and Johnson discuss the "moral" of *Othello,* a conversation which suggests that even in the eighteenth century sophisticated discussions of literature embraced the didactic view of literature and look for a "moral":

> I [BOSWELL] observed that the great defect of the tragedy of *Othello* was that it had no moral, for that no man could resist the circumstances of suspicion which are artfully suggested to Othello's mind. JOHNSON: "In the first place, Sir, we learn from *Othello* this very useful moral, not to make an unequal match; in the second place, we learn not to yield too readily to suspicion."

The evident difficulty of attempting to reduce so powerful a literary work to a "moral" such as Johnson suggested and which Boswell was looking for but could not find, will be apparent, and Johnson's serious attempt is not much less ludicrous than Thomas Rymer's sarcastic observation that the "moral" of *Othello* is that "ladies should look to their linen."

The point I should like to make is that the moral force of *Othello* does not and cannot depend upon finding a "moral" in the play, but more nearly upon Shakespeare's success in generating the judicial emotions of sympathy and antipathy toward the characters.

A useful way of measuring the degree of sympathy and antipathy for the characters in a story might be to draw a diagram on which could be projected the characters in accordance with how much sympathy or antipathy they evoke. Such a line might look something like this, if it were drawn for the main characters in Shakespeare's *Othello*:

100% Sympathetic			100% Unsympathetic
Desdemona	Othello		Iago

There would, I think, be no disputing the placing of Desdemona on or at the 100 percent sympathetic end of the scale since she dies a wholly innocent death, nor Iago as the utter villain at the other end of the line. The audience thus experiences the judicial emotions which Shakespeare intended. It is perhaps arguable that Othello should be regarded as more sympathetic than this diagram suggests or perhaps less so, and I do not propose to discuss the problem here; but the most interesting and often the most important characters are those for whom the reader experiences mixed feelings.

Other characters in *Othello* such as Cassio and Roderigo and Brabantio and Emelia could also be placed on this line in accordance with what Shakespeare intended the audience to feel toward them. Tragedy, as Aristotle insisted, characteristically portrays the tragic hero as neither totally sympathetic nor totally unsympathetic, but somewhere in between, because, although he is culpable, and hence to a degree unsympathetic, he also suffers in excess of what he deserves, and thus warrants a degree of sympathy.

To cite another example, Milton's God and Satan in *Paradise Lost* may perhaps provide the broadest possible spectrum of the sympathy-antipathy line. Adam and Eve, by virtue of their inherent goodness and willful badness, belong, like tragic characters, somewhere toward the middle. Milton's God and Satan also represent the characters with the greatest possible capacities for good and evil respectively, a fact which makes them more *awesome* characters than any others in all literature, and which contributes much to the grandeur and magnificence of the poem.

*****

I should like to dwell for a moment on this phenomenon of awe because the emotion of awe has the effect of heightening the judicial emotions of sympathy and antipathy. It is the emotion the audience experiences out of the recognition that the hero has greater capacities by virtue of his or her station, character, strength, or a host of other characteristics which make one person greater or better than another. The emotion of awe emphasizes at least the political superiority of the great king over the common reader or spectator and can therefore increase his sympathy for the deeds or the plight of the great king even while experiencing the exultation which comes from identifying with him. History-making events celebrated in epic poems inevitably evoke awe for the hero as is so evidently the case with classical heroes like Odysseus, Achilles, and Aeneas, and with medieval and Renaissance epic heroes like Beowulf and Orlando.

Traditionally awe has also been a crucial ingredient of true tragedy. Aristotle had insisted that tragic heroes "must be illustrious"; and being "illustrious," they necessarily invite awe. The tragedies of Aeschylus,

Sophocles, and Euripides, for example, depict awesome tragic heroes, as do almost all Renaissance tragedies. Italian Renaissance critics in particular insisted upon the phenomenon of awe in tragedy, and the tradition was practiced in Elizabethan tragedy. There were, it is true, excursions into domestic tragedy," such as Shakespeare's *Romeo and Juliet*, Heywood's *A Woman Killed with Kindness*, and in the eighteenth century in plays like George Lillo's *The London Merchant* (which Voltaire called "a tradesman's tragedy").

But such a concept of tragedy was not yet the norm. The practice of making the tragic hero awesome was still regarded as an integral part of the tragic pleasure, as Aristotle defined it, and very often he was an historical character as well. Even the closet drama tradition in the nineteenth century represented by Shelley, Byron, and Browning among others, carried on the tradition of awesome tragic heroes.

But the depiction of supremely wicked characters can also provoke awe, including wicked kings. Milton had to deal with the problem of awe in Satan in the first two books of *Paradise Lost*, and hence left himself open, however unjustly, to the charge of sympathizing with Satan, or even of making him the real hero of the poem. This ability of the author of a tragedy or epic poem to instill awe in his audience is one of the ways in which the literary experience exalts or even inspires the reader, and it is all the more powerful because it communicates this admiration not through mere reason, which appeals only to the understanding, but through the emotions and hence reaches the will, which more nearly determines human behavior, and therefore heightens the moral force of the literary work.

It would seem to follow, then, that those who, like George Lillo and Arthur Miller, attempt to demonstrate that prentices and salesmen can be quite as powerful tragic figures as kings, have a good deal to answer for. It may be difficult to show that a tragedy, for example like Lillo's *The London Merchant* or Arthur Miller's own *Death of a Salesman* exerts as powerful a moral effect upon an audience as say *Oedipus Rex* or *Othello*. In his own defense Arthur Miller observed, "I believe that the common man is as apt a subject for tragedy in its highest sense as kings were. On the face of it," he continues, "this ought to be obvious in the light of modern psychiatry, which bases its analysis upon classical formulations, such as Oedipus or Orestes complexes, for instance, which were enacted by royal beings, but which apply to everyone in similar emotional situations." This is an old controversy, and I do not wish to enter into it here except to observe that no amount of psychiatry will make Oedipus or Othello less awesome or allow George Barnwell or Willie Loman to be more awesome; and if awe does heighten the emotional and moral effect of a tragedy, then tradesmen and salesmen are bound to lose out.

In any case, what I wish to emphasize is that in any serious story whatsoever, the characters, on the basis of what they are and what they do, if reflecting moral intent, inescapably evoke the judicial emotions of sympathy or antipathy in the reader, and that these emotions form the basis of the moral force of the story. Therefore a sympathy-antipathy line for any serious story, whether in the form of epic, tragedy, comedy, or anything in between whether told, acted out or portrayed on the screen, would make sense and would illustrate the phenomenon I am trying to describe. In some stories the characters may be all sympathetic, in others all unsympathetic, and in others a combination of both with varying degrees in the range of sympathetic and unsympathetic characters; so that the moral force of virtually every serious story whatsoever can be "graphically" displayed on the sympathy-antipathy line by the fact that it seriously evokes these judicial emotions. The disagreements are likely to arise from determining just where on the sympathy-antipathy line each character belongs; and that, as I shall suggest, can be a problem. The pattern of the line can vary from story to story, but it will be there, however subtle the author may be, and even how unconsciously the author may have evoked these emotions.

Theoretically it would not be possible to place a character in the story on the point separating the sympathy from the antipathy side unless he made no moral decision in the play, in which case the reader would have no judicial emotional reaction, and the character would contribute nothing to the moral force of the play, as for example, a servant who merely announces the arrival of a guest.

It may be observed that after the Renaissance there was a gradual trend in serious stories, whatever form they took, either to reduce the role of the villain or eventually to eliminate him altogether. This development had the effect of reducing the range of sympathetic and unsympathetic characters, particularly in the newly-arrived genre of the novel, so that in the eighteenth century, instead of the portrayal of characters ranging in sympathy and antipathy from Iago and Desdemona, the portrayal often ranged no farther than from Parson Adams to Blifil in Fielding's *Tom Jones*. And in the later nineteenth century the range often became even smaller. Dickens' villains become almost an anachronism. In serious twentieth century literature, with notable and wondrous exceptions, the villain has disappeared altogether.

In fact, in twentieth century literature it very often happens that characters who would once have been regarded as unsympathetic, even satirical, suddenly, or fairly suddenly, become sometimes sympathetic, and even sometimes heroes. Edmund Fuller in *Man and Modern Fiction* called attention to the phenomenon of the lovable bum in early twentieth century literature and how he was in later twentieth century novels transformed into the jolly slasher, the fun-loving dope pusher, and the genial rapist. And in twentieth century drama, instead of getting tragic heroes of the stature of Oedipus or Othello, we get not merely "tragic" figures like Arthur Miller's salesman, but the derelicts of Eugene O'Neill's *The Iceman Cometh* and neanderthal types in his *Desire under the Elms*, and perhaps even more extreme, the miserable wretches of Gorky's *The Lower Depths*, all of whom may be said to evoke not awe but reverse awe.

This phenomenon of elevating "low" characters regarded as unsympathetic or comic during the Middle Ages and Renaissance into sympathetic or even tragic characters during the course of the last two centuries, has major implications for the moral force of literature, and would appear to reduce it in modern literature generally, with, however, notable exceptions. Essentially the problem is that many literary works from the middle of the eighteenth century onward are open to the charge of being sentimental, more specifically beginning with Sir Richard Steele in comedies like *The Conscious Lovers*, in tragedies like George Lillo's *The London Merchant,* and in the novel from the beginning, i.e., with Richardson and Fielding.

What is there about the phenomenon of sentimentality that creates problems in the moral effect of literary works which exhibit it? First of all, what is sentimentality? It may be defined briefly as the attempt of an author to get his audience to evoke more sympathy for a character than the character deserves. Wherever this phenomenon occurs, then the excessive degree of sympathy evoked for the character constitutes what might be called the *unjust feeling*, as opposed to what Yvor Winters calls *the just feeling*. When an author evokes the just feeling, it means that he has evoked the proper degree of sympathy or antipathy proper not only according to the author's own lights but also the reader's lights. It is the degree of sympathy or antipathy that the reader feels is due the character ,and he therefore agrees with the author's attitude toward the character. If, however, the reader feels that the author is trying to get him to feel more sympathy (or occasionally more antipathy) toward the character than is warranted, then the author is open to the charge of evoking the unjust feeling; and since the just feeling is a judicial and hence a moral feeling, then the unjust feeling is an immoral feeling. This phenomenon then leads to the conclusion that sentimentality is essentially an immoral feeling, and therefore results in at least a blemished story and at worst a profoundly immoral story.

Why, then, is sentimentality an unjust and hence an immoral feeling? The answer seems to be that it distorts, indeed corrupts the emotions, or even misplaces them. Let me try to illustrate how the experience of sentimentality could have a deleterious effect upon the emotions of the audience. Suppose, for example, that someone is watching a movie about the dog Lassie, whom a bad man threw rocks at, causing her great pain and anguish so that she has to limp throughout the whole movie, and is finally killed off when she is run over by a drunk driver. This phenomenon can be so touching that a member of the audience is moved to tears and continues crying even after leaving the theater. Suppose too that as he comes out of the theater he sees a legless beggar, hat in hand, in the street. It just may be that the moved movie-goer, having used up all his sympathy on Lassie, might, as he approaches the beggar, kick him over into the gutter instead of dropping a quarter into his hat. The example is, of course, far-fetched, but it illustrates perhaps as well as any how a sentimental indulgence can distort moral values by not leaving enough emotional energy to exercise it where it belongs.

In order to illustrate the phenomenon of sentimentality graphically in a story, it is possible to use the sympathy-antipathy line again, but in a different way. Actually, what is required is two lines, namely the author's line and the reader's or spectator's line. Let us say that the first line is the author's line and the reader places the character X where he thinks the author wants him to be placed. The second line indicates where the reader himself thinks he should be placed. If there is a discrepancy, then the lines might look something like this:

100% Sympathetic   100% Unsympathetic

Author's Line

_____X_____|_____

Reader's Line

_____X__|_____

|—————————|
(tabular difference)

The tabular difference is the disagreement between the author and reader in their emotional judgment of the character and would thus be a measure of sentimentality evoked by the author, and it would also be a measure of the extent of the unjust or immoral feeling. If the X's appear on opposite sides of the center line, then something is seriously wrong, either with the author's writing or the reader's reading. One does not, of course, measure sentimentality with calipers, but some general understanding of the problem of sentimentality in a literary work under suspicion can from this example be thus obtained.

What is hoped for, of course, is that the author's emotional judgment and the reader's emotional judgment will coincide, or nearly so, so that there is no consequential tabular difference and so that the just feeling can be achieved. Now for many if not most readers, detecting sentimentality in a story is not easy, and if the author is skillful enough it may be very difficult even for a seasoned reader to detect, and in fact may require the greatest strain on one's literary intelligence. There is no shortage of sentimental artistic works in the nineteenth and twentieth century to practice on, works even by serious authors, for there is now a tradition of it that has lasted for more than two centuries. Sentimentality appears not only on Mother's Day cards but in the movie theaters, in novels, both serious and frivolous, on the stage, and in poetry and in painting, music, and the other arts as well. In fact it may be said to permeate American culture.

*****

Without dwelling on the causes of widespread sentimentality in literature, on the screen and in the arts generally, it may be said that the chief cause is the rise of the popularity of the idea of the natural goodness of man, which, in the intellectual history of the Western World, did not really take hold until the eighteenth century, but it has been with us ever since. The idea of the natural goodness of man is a great leveler not only because it seems to make every person morally equal to every other, but because it also tends to take away the whole idea of moral responsibility and culpability by placing the blame for immoral actions on the environment, or on some biological or hereditary or psychiatric or almost any other cause over which the "victim" has no control. It is this phenomenon perhaps more than any other that has caused the villain to disappear from serious modern literature and explains why the range of sympathetic and unsympathetic characters in most modern stories has shrunk and even become distorted. In Steinbeck's *The Grapes of Wrath,* for example, the Joads and all their friends are essentially intended to be sympathetic; only groups—like cops, rich-bastards, fruit growers, landowners and bankers—are villains, and none of them have names. When one of the Okies asks, "Who can we shoot?" it turns out that there is no one to shoot. They are all so much victims of the "system" that despite the penchant of some of them for stealing, whoring, boozing, and murdering, the reader may feel ashamed that he is not one of them. *The Grapes of Wrath* is a powerful artistic achievement, so that the sentimentality of it makes the unjust feeling (i.e., the immoral feeling) which it produces, all the more powerful.

In the literature written since about 1750, the problem of sentimentality is ubiquitous, and the closer the literature is to the present time the greater the problem is likely to be. It could be said by way of contrast, that before 1700, sentimentality in the great literature of Western civilization is much more rarely a problem, chiefly because the idea of the natural culpability of man held sway over the idea of the natural goodness of man, so that emotions of sympathy and antipathy could be more justly conveyed. One of the great tasks of the *literateur* is to find great works after 1750 that are not sentimental; there are a good many of them because not all writers have been profoundly influenced by the idea of the natural goodness of man or by deterministic philosophical systems, but they sometimes need to be ferreted out.

But who is to say whether the judicial feelings evoked by characters in stories are just or unjust? Ideally they would provoke the same *universal* emotional response, i.e., the same response that anyone in virtually any culture not only worldwide but timewide would experience or as nearly so as possible. What is hoped for in literature is that universal actions provoke the same universal emotions. It has been widely agreed that all of the world's great religions support many of the same basic moral principles, and that therefore the sympathy and antipathy emanating from these principles would be universally alike or at least similar. There are perhaps few who regard hatred, jealousy adultery, robbery, theft, and murder as moral ideals either in religion or out of it And the list could be extended much farther. Similarly, a list of desirable traits, like kindness, generosity, sacrificial love, honesty, and truthfulness are ideas which are more or less universally approved. But in general the more universal the emotional reaction to the characters in a literary work the greater the potential universal value of the work.

If all the readers of a literary work are conditioned by the moral values of Christianity —even without the   theology of Christianity —the problem of achieving a just feeling among the characters in stories is made easier.

But the best evidence of the extent to which sympathy and antipathy may be universally and uniformly said to be evoked for the characters in a literary work does not come from syllogisms. Let a group of people from around the world gather in one and room and read, say, Shakespeare's *King Lear* with comprehension in order to determine which characters are sympathetic and which are not. How much disagreement would there be, for example, in their attitude toward the villainy of Goneril and Regan and Edmund, and how much sympathy for the goodness of Edgar and Cordelia, and how much sympathy for the suffering, if erring, Lear? Are there not dozens or hundreds of other major literary works in which the same, or essentially the same universal feelings for the characters could be achieved?

Where the sympathy and antipathy of the reader do not concide with those of the author, there may be a variety of causes. The chief one, as I have suggested, may be the philosophical disagreements over the moral nature of man, which is the main cause of sentimentality in literature, as in the arts generally. The unjust feeling may also be the result of the primacy of ideological premises either on the part of the author or the reader, so that the ideological thinking of the character—or of the author—may be incompatible with that of the reader. The author's liberal or conservative orientation, for example, may clash with that of the reader, so that he might evaluate the actions of the same characters differently. Cultural differences, or even personal experience, could also help account for problems in experiencing the just feeling. In any case, something of the universal moral value of the literary work is lost wherever the unjust feeling prevails, particularly if the author, rather than the reader, is responsible for narrowing it.

It is the reader's task—and the critic's task—therefore, to determine whether or not the just feeling has been conveyed. If the conclusion is that it has not, then the reader and critic should stick to their own principles and declare that the author, not they, are at fault. The reader in effect judges the author's judgment and should have the last word, and that judgment is a crucial part of the genuinely critical process. In contemplating a sentimental work the reader does not have to grant the author his *donnée*, his premise; he has every right to question the author's premise, particularly about his view of human nature, which produced the sentimentality in the first place.

Generally the more complex the actions and general behavior and values of the characters in questions are, the more difficult it is to measure and identify the just feeling. And yet it seems fair to say that there should be at least a core of emotional agreement for most characters in most literary works, and that fact alone would be enough to establish the validity of the concept of the just feeling, as well as that of the unjust feeling.

Such, then, is a brief and admittedly simplified solution to the problem of how literature can be moral without having a moral, how it "edifies," how, to use Horace's term, it "instructs."

*****

The second half of Horace's formula, namely how literature "delights" is no less complex, but the history of criticism has been more successful in explaining that phenomenon, and readers who like to read literature don't need to be persuaded that literature delights. An obvious source of the pleasure of literature comes from the phenomenon which permits the reader by a pure act of imagination to experience vicariously the emotions which the characters experience, such as grief, sadness, anger, fear, hatred, love, jealousy, envy or a host of other emotions, which, when experienced in real life, have uncomfortable consequences. This sort of pleasure, which strikes close to the heart of the literary experience, enables the reader to enjoy the pleasures of the emotional life without its pains, and to expand the range and kind of emotions, as well as experiences, which real life cannot, or does not, provide.

It is possible to argue, in fact, as Joseph Addison did, that the pleasures of the printed page exceed the pleasures of the visual arts. Addison pointed out in *The Spectator Papers* (No. 416) that statuary is less pleasurable than painting because the beholder exercises his imagination to perceive a third dimension, which a statue already provides, and that literature, not supplying any visual help, relies wholly upon the imagination, which being more fully exercised, produces greater pleasure. Whether or not Addison is right about the relative pleasures of statuary and painting, his argument for the superiority and more intense pleasure of literature, precisely because the imagination is fully engaged, seems quite plausible. Those who deny the validity of Addison's argument may be charged with an underdeveloped imagination, or an insensitivity to language, both of which mark deficiencies in the reader rather than in the literature.

Another source of the great pleasure of stories comes from the fact that the reader is invited to sympathize with the characters, or not to sympathize, as the case may be. Thus the emotions involving non-identification, which, as we have seen, provide the chief moral force of literature, are also a source of delight. The reader somehow takes pleasure in feeling sorry for the right characters and in hating the right characters. One controversial explanation for this phenomenon is that a story provides the reader with an opportunity to exercise his sado-masochistic instincts, the masochistic pleasure from identifying with the suffering hero, and his sadistic instincts from non-identification, which allow him to enjoy the character's suffering. Not everyone will admit that sado-masochistic instincts are natural to mankind, and so they may well find this theory abhorrent. Unlike the non-identifying emotions, which are experienced for all characters in a story who demonstrate moral intent, identifying emotions are highly selective. On the assumption that the reader instinctively does not identify with characters who are worse than he, in satirical comedies like Jonson's *The Alchemist* or Gogol's *The Inspector General,* there would presumably be no identifying emotions at all, for all, or virtually all, the characters are rogues. In a romantic comedy, identification with the lovers is more certain unless they too are being satirized. Pleasure comes from feeling superior to characters whom the reader regards as inferior, especially on intellectual or moral grounds; though, as we have seen, many modern writers invite the reader to identify with such characters whether the reader is inclined to or not.

It is perhaps in epic poetry and tragedy that identification or empathy is the most emotionally powerful. The reader readily identifies with the epic hero, and much of the pleasure comes from the vicarious experience of seeming, for a time, to be that awesome character. The same may be said of tragic heroes, because emotional involvement with them is above all what the tragic writer seeks. Aristotle considered tragedy to be a higher literary form than the epic because the emotional involvement is more intense, and hence more pleasurable.

Whether a reader can identify with more than one character in a story may be debatable, though it would seem as though he could, at least when the characters are not immediately interacting among themselves. It can probably be argued that the reader experiences more pleasure in identifying with a character who, as Aristotle said, is "better" than the reader or spectator than the same as he is, since identifying with a character like oneself deprives the reader or spectator of an exalting experience rather than an ordinary one. In satirical comedy, no identification takes place, at least with the satirical characters or "low" characters in any kind of comedy. The pleasure of comedy most often comes precisely from feeling superior to the characters. But as is well known, the novel from the beginning tended to present characters "like" the reader or sometimes "worse" than the reader, so that novels with awesome characters are fairly rare and in the drama beginning especially with Ibsen they became increasingly rare. And the experience of identifying with an awesome character, whether in the modern novel or modern drama, is almost universally denied the reader for reasons which I have already indicated. It is likely to be experienced chiefly in those novels or plays which portray historical characters. But the main point is that this ability to identify with a character in a story is a source of powerful pleasure, and offers the vicarious opportunity of experiencing the entire spectrum of emotions, and with impunity.

One of the intriguing questions concerning the emotional effect of a story is how vicariously experiencing powerful and painful emotions produces pleasure. David Hume attempted to answer the question as it concerns the powerful emotions evoked by tragedy, and concluded that "the force of imagination, the energy of expression, the power of numbers [i.e., the verbal rhythms], the charms of imitation; all these are naturally, of themselves delightful to the mind. And when the object presented lays hold also of some affection [i.e., emotion] the pleasure still rises upon us by the conversion of this subordinate movement into that which is predominant. The passion, though perhaps natural, and when excited by the simple appearance of a real object it may be painful; yet is so smoothed and softened, and mollified when raised by the finer arts, then it affords the highest entertainment."

Aristotle observed that the pleasures of literature come in part from the extension of pleasure of imitation to the pleasure of observing imitation, and that further pleasure comes from the "harmony" that is produced from the arrangement of the words and the sequence of events.

But in general it may be said that the sources of pleasure from a story, whether it is dramatized or narrated, are legion, and range from the aesthetic perception of its form, the beauty of its plot, the nature and variety of the characters, what they say and how they say it, the pleasures of the imagination itself, and the rhetorical pleasures which come from the style, even down to the most incidental felicities of expression. All together they make up a combination of pleasures that can surpass the pleasure of any other experience with written or spoken words. The pleasures of story-telling, particularly in the hands of a great writer are undisputed, and I will not therefore discuss the nature or the cause of them further. The main problem with which this chapter is charged is not how literature "delights," but how it "instructs."

To summarize: The novelist or the dramatist has the obligation (1) to create a story in such a way as to permit the reader to achieve as high a degree of empathy as possible, and (2) to judge the characters by eliciting from the audience the degree of sympathy or antipathy which he feels the reader ought to experience. If the author's descriptions of human experience are *convincing*, then the story can provide a powerful moral and aesthetic experience which cannot be had in any other way. The author thus becomes the "teacher" and the audience his "students," for authors know or should know how much sympathy or antipathy his characters, performing representative actions, deserve. One of the first duties of the true critic, the judicial critic, then, is to determine whether the sympathy or antipathy which the author generates toward the characters is warranted. What the reader—and the critic—hope for is that the author's judgment of the characters produces the just feeling toward each of the characters. In a sense, then, the best literature may be said to have the ability to *condition* the will, because it appeals to the proper emotions based upon the actions, good or bad, of the characters. And since it is possible to have an exquisite understanding of the wrongness or rightness of an action, and still perform it or not perform it anyway simply because the understanding, not the will has been touched, it would appear that these methods of arriving at truth which reach the will are the most powerful. Religion can perhaps do it best, but literature next best.

*****

It is pertinent here also to inquire into the extent to which the simultaneous phenomenon of identification and non-identification occur also in lyric poetry. Analyzing the emotional and moral effects of lyric poetry is somewhat different from that of story-telling, whether in verse or prose, because lyric poetry lacks the plot and character which are crucial to stories (and narrative poems) and which are major sources of emotion. It must instead rely more upon statement and the emotional reaction to statement, so that individual lines, phrases, and words carry a heavier burden in determining emotional reaction than they do in the story-teller's art. It may be said that the emotional experience provided by a lyric poem generally involves far more identification than non-identification. This is not to say that the emotion of sympathy or even antipathy may not be involved, but they seem to play a lesser role than the emotions which come from empathy, i.e., the experience of feeling the same way as the poet. An illustration from a children's poem may help. In this stanza from a poem by Robert Louis Stevenson (to keep the discussion simple) both sympathy and empathy seem clearly to be evoked:

> And does it not seem hard to you ,
> When all the sky is clear and blue,
> And I should like só much to play
> To have to go to bed by day?

A child reading the poem can sympathize knowing that the child in the poem would rather be playing outside than having to take a nap. Similarly the child reader is made capable of feeling the same emotions as the child in the poem, which in this instance may be not so much indignation as longing. Whatever name the emotion evokes, the audience can feel it.

In lyric poetry, the emotions which the poet communicates should be *motivated* emotions, i.e., there should be good and comprehensible reason for them, as in this little poem by Stevenson. Unmotivated emotions are essentially unrefined emotions, whereas refined emotions depend upon proper motivation in poetry and in the arts generally. In real life, on the other hand, everyone at one time or another has experienced emotions which cannot be accounted for.

The phenomenon of non-identification may not be so marked as it is in Stevenson's poem, but by virtue of the intensity of the emotion with which the reader can identify, lyric poetry can be a powerful emotional experience not only because of its brevity, but also its form, its language, its rhythms, and all the other peculiar characteristics due a lyric poem. But just as with story-telling there is still the question of whether the emotion expressed is a just emotion, and therefore whether the just feeling has been achieved; for the just feeling is quite as important in a lyric poem as in a novel or a play.

Ben Jonson may have been right in declaring that "a poet is not born every year"; but even if one were born only every other year there would still be some 300 great lyric poets since the time of Petrarch, and those poets, however one may identify them, have provided us with some of the most powerful aesthetic experiences through their use of words that man is capable of. In short spaces they are able to refine both our moral and aesthetic sensibilities, of refining our emotional life, of enriching our awareness of human experience, of properly conditioning our will—not merely our understanding—of offering us new perceptions, of enabling us to discover new values, and all the while providing an intensely pleasurable or at least a valuable emotional experience.

*****

Whether imaginative literature is in the form of fiction, drama, or lyric poetry, its real power and service to mankind is perhaps best understood in light of the fact that man, whatever else he is, is an emotional animal. And it may well be that managing one's emotions is the ultimate key to happiness. Surely one of the hard facts of life is that not wealth nor comfort nor success nor personal achievement can teach us how to manage our emotions. Aristotle supposed that managing one's emotions is primarily an act of reason and that the study of philosophy was the way to achieve it. So too, apparently, did Plato. But it may be that in this they were both wrong. It is literature not philosophy or history and certainly not mathematics or the sciences (none of the sciences) which can most effectively manage our emotions. Certainly raw experience of life rarely helps. The raw experience of life is more likely to provide opportunities to abuse or misuse the emotions rather than to control them or to refine them, and hence to be a major cause of unhappiness.

Literature can also expand our emotional experience by offering us opportunities to enjoy vicariously actions which would otherwise be closed to us. And for those who are truly print-oriented, the artistic written words give access to a kind and intensity of pleasure which no audio-visual media, including the other fine arts, can afford because the powers and pleasure of the verbal imagination are more fully employed. Evidence for this phenomenon can readily be found in reading a story to even a four-year-old child, who, all wide-eyed, lets his imagination roam unfettered as he hears about what giants and princes and fairies and ogres do and as he learns how to hate the villains and not only to love but *to be* the heroes or heroines. Subtler and even more valuable emotional experiences are open to adults who read great novels and poems and see the best plays which are the products of the literary imagination of writers of genius.

The literary imagination, then, both on the part of the writer and the reader, has thus good claim to being among the most powerful, most fruitful, and most useful of all the peculiarly human gifts with which men and women are endowed. Where in the world of words, one may finally ask, is anyone to find its equal?

Chapter VI

Can Literature Survive?

If literature is as *potentially* powerful a social and moral force as I have suggested and as history from the time of the ancient Greeks has insisted; and if it has been trivialized in the twentieth century, particularly in America, as this study has tried to show, what, then, are its prospects? For the foreseeable future, forces which are now militating against literature, such as those which I have identified in the first four chapters, are likely to intensify rather than abate. In fact, it is not easy to imagine a scenario which would bring it back to the popularity and the dignity which it enjoyed in the nineteenth century or even the earlier twentieth century.

If literature is to thrive or even survive, it is evident, first of all, that a print-oriented culture must also survive. But there seems no doubt that the authority of the written word is being assaulted from all sides: from the steady increase in illiteracy and semi-literacy, from the incursions of audio-visual technologies, from the development of educational theories which increasingly de-emphasize the importance of the written word, and even in the universities, where literary and epistemological theories often denigrate the written word in general and literature in particular. A print-oriented society depends primarily upon the schools' turning out print-oriented students, and with it to teach students to read and to respect, if not love the best literature. But more and more they are turning out what I have called audio-visual students, students whose education is based more upon what they see and hear than upon what they read, to the point that they frequently become habituated, even addicted to sights and sounds and increasingly allergic to what they read, even when the know how to read. As one of the characters in the comic strip *Peanuts* declares, "I never read anything!!! If it isn't on video, forget it!!!"

But the problem for the schools is not so much that they are more and more imposing audio-visual technology upon students as a substitute for the written word; it is that they do not teach them to read well enough to enable them to experience the delights of the written word. As I indicated in Chapter III of this study, the overriding problem is that the look-say method and the "whole language" method, instead of a systematic phonics method, have become so thoroughly institutionalized by the educational establishment, i.e., by the professors of education and their chief pedagogical organization, the National Education Association (NEA), that not even a bloodless revolution is likely to be enough to reform the reading program in most schools in the country. The best hope is that methods of teaching reading will become a political problem, as they have in California, and that the state governments or the city governments will override the educational establishment and force them to reinstitute systematic phonics in the classroom. Such political interference, however abhorrent, may be the only way out. Otherwise, one may predict with unswerving confidence that the massive failure to teach students to read will be at least as serious a problem in 25 years as it is now.

Given the sacrosanct methods and materials from which students try to learn in most of our schools the reading levels would not improve significantly even if we were able suddenly to wipe out the wide range of problems commonly blamed for the poor reading achievements among students, problems such as overcrowded classrooms, poverty, high dropout rates, family difficulties, and peculiarly American epidemics of dyslexia. It is not easy to envision a time when many elementary or even some high school students will become good enough readers to comprehend easily the passages from the nineteenth and early twentieth century fifth and sixth grade readers which appear in Chapter III of this study. They will be doing well to read with some degree of proficiency the often sorry selections in their modern readers. As a result of the continuing reading problems which most elementary school students suffer from, there is no reason to suppose in the decade or decades ahead that the watered-down, undistinguished, up-to-the-minute reading selections taught in the middle schools will be consequentially improved in the future, and they may well become even worse. In turn, the literary limbo to which these students are consigned does not prepare them to read truly high quality literature in the high schools, even when they are offered the opportunity.

There is commonly a confusion between the student who is truly literate and the student who is only semi-literate, for often the assumption is that if the student can read at whatever elementary level he is therefore literate. But there are degrees and degrees of semi-literacy, which are not often distinguished. The truly literate student is very literate indeed.

*****

It is true that a good many high schools in the country, especially in private and suburban systems, still offer students a decent literary education, though more and more they have to scramble for suitable anthologies without having to resort to a series of paperback books, which, however excellent in themselves, contribute to the destruction of a canon of literary selections or at least authors whose greatness is undisputed, and the study of whose works can therefore provide a common literary heritage that can do much to maintain cultural unity in this country.

But most students, if they study literature at all, seem destined to continue reading third-and fourth-rate novels and plays and poems of the kind they are exposed to now, even in some weak anthologies, and students will continue to be intimidated by good poetry because they no longer read it in the elementary grades. Updated literature anthologies of the quality of the one entitled *From Beowulf to Thomas Hardy*, so widely used earlier in the century, are hardly likely to return.

But even worse than the multitude of semi-literates in the country is the phenomenon that many, perhaps most, of those who can understand and enjoy good literature don't read any more of it than do the semi-literates. This development bodes particularly ill for the future fortunes of literature because it suggests that fully literate people find something better, or at least easier to do than to read good novels and stories and poems. Most mystery stories and romances do not really qualify, though reading second- and third-rate fiction is better than reading no fiction. In fact, it seems likely that most college graduates and indeed many with advanced degrees are among the unreading readers. One sometimes hears that a college graduate is "widely read," but we need to hear more often about the college graduate who is "narrowly read." The narrowly-read person who holds a position of responsibility in politics or in the professions or in business, for that matter, is more often than not likely to be less valuable and less competent than his well-read counterpart.

And what does it mean to be widely read? It means above all wide reading in literature and history and philosophy, not merely widely read in what Sir Philip Sidney called the "serving sciences," as opposed to the humanities. Erasmus once observed that "experience is the schoolhouse of fools," implying that much can be learned by reading and hence by profiting from the wisdom and mistakes of others. By this measure, good literature stands to be the greatest provider of wisdom about human nature, combining as it does the universal actions of people together with an emotional judgment of these actions, in a way that history and philosophy, as we have seen, cannot.

Unfortunately the kind of education that most college students now get goes a long way toward guaranteeing that they will emerge at the end of four years among the narrowly read, including particularly those who major in such areas as business administration, education, communications, and dozens of other areas which do much to guarantee a narrow reading experience, especially when the core of the curriculum is soggy or non-existent, and the trend seems to be toward making it more soggy, not less. The narrowly-read college graduate, then, signals an ill omen for the prospects of the humanities, including literature, for if the college graduate does not continue to read literature, then who will? And yet this emphasis upon a servile education (as opposed to a liberal education) seems destined to continue as long as the demand for narrowly-based careerism continues to intensify.

*****

But the last remaining fortress of literature is the English departments of the nation's colleges and universities. This fortress too, as we have seen, appears to be crumbling. The big guns of the fortress, the ones with the greatest power and range, namely the literary theorists, are misfiring and even backfiring. Virtually all of them, as I have indicated in Chapter II of this study, are energetically engaged in one way or another in trivializing the literary arts, and even theorizing about their irrelevance.

What can be expected of them in the future? The short answer seems to be more misfiring and backfiring, perhaps until the entire fortress is destroyed. In Chapter II, I divided these most highly influential theorists into three groups: the dessicators, the politicizors and the destructors. There are few of those whose writing and thinking today do not fit one of these three categories. To summarize briefly, the dessicators are those who seek after every imaginable fact that a literary work will yield usually for the sake of the fact, whether it is psychological, historical, biographical, anthropological, or rhetorical, with little or no attention to the total aesthetic and moral effect of the literary work upon the audience. The politicizors approach a literary work as primarily a political document, and praise or blame it for its political or social orientation, again with minimal attention to its artistic excellence or lack thereof. The destructors attack the validity of the very language which makes up the literary work and deny that it is possible for the writer to communicate to the reader because words are abstract and conceptual, and the audience can communicate accurately only through the concrete and perceptual. All three are profoundly anti-humanistic in that they are not at all concerned with what literature does best, namely communicate through words universal human experiences and truths by evoking emotions proper to the characters of the narrative or the author of the lyric poem.

The question concerning literary theory, then, is which of these three will succeed in outstripping the other two in influence. At the present time the outcome is uncertain. The Modern Language Association meetings, where literary scholars and critics gather annually, is perhaps the best bellwether, and thus provides a portent for literary studies in the future. One can begin to discern from these meetings that the politicizors are pulling ahead of the dessicators and destructors. The destructors appear to be choking on their own absurdities. Deconstructionists are already beginning to deconstruct the work of other deconstrutionists, and may be expected in time to self-destruct as they are already doing in France, where deconstructionism was born . They are in direct defiance of the common sense and experience of almost everybody, which tells them that words do communicate truths and that they communicate the same thing, or enough of the same thing, to an audience so that the pursuit of the written word in general and literature in particular is still a worthwhile, even exalted endeavor. The dessicators also seem to be losing out by virtue of the fact that the have never seriously addressed the crucial question of what literature is for. Having rejected the two-thousand-year-old answer that its purpose is the moral effect upon the reader, they have retreated into their own peculiar little worlds seeking facts and studying rhetorical structures and leaving to others the question of what it's all for. The very sterility of their work will guarantee its eventual demise.

The politicizors, on the other had, have moved in to fill the vacuum, for they feel strongly that the best purpose to which literature can be put is to promote political and social reforms, especially radical liberal reforms. They are therefore not only a loud voice but a pervasive voice at MLA meetings, and it is not too much to say that they dominate them. It is not only the feminists, but the Neo-Marxists, the New Historicists, the gays, the lesbians, the multiculturalists, and a wide assortment of other and less compelling special interest groups who are making the biggest splash. If one were obliged to choose the leader among them at present, the dominant group might well be the feminists. The Marxists seem to be losing influence if only because they must face the reality of the fate of Marxism. But Marxist literary theory still hangs on among literary critics and hence also in MLA programs. Other special interest groups among the politicizors are probably too specialized to have a great deal of influence, except the multiculturists, who appear to be rising fast. But the feminists, claiming as they do to represent half of the human race, plead the feminist cause with conviction, some would say a stridency, that sometimes drowns out all rivals.

If the theories of contemporary critics and scholars were confined within the walls of the MLA hotels where they meet, their theorizing might remain relatively harmless, but these theories are being put into practice in college classrooms, where literary works are more and more being examined primarily for the author's attitude toward gender, race, class, and ethnicity, rather than for their literary excellence or for their contribution to an understanding of the entire human species. This preoccupation is now leading some influential universities to a reassessment of the entire core curriculum in favor of political correctness and multiculturalism and to a revolution in whatever is left of the literary canon. The idea that students should study a common body of literature or at least of authors is no longer imperative, and for some not even desirable. In fact our whole literary heritage is under attack by the politicizors, who want their own political, racial, social, sexual, and cultural views reflected in the literature which they assign students to read. And since they rarely find these views expressed in much of the literature from Homer to about the middle of the nineteenth century or later, the increasing practice is to replace the timeless with the timely, which in turn means phasing out the classics in favor of not merely modern literature but contemporary literature which is sensitive to current political, social, sexual, racial, ethnic, and other narrowly-based criteria, the relative literary value of which can be, and often is, in serious doubt.

This movement is growing rapidly, and those who oppose it are either becoming fewer or at least less vocal, so that political radicalism is more and more having its way in literature classrooms at the college level. Even Homer's and Shakespeare's works are on the endangered list; or where the traditionally great literature before 1800, or even 1900, is still being studied, it is being increasingly subject to "re-interpretation" in the light of whatever political or social agenda professors are currently pushing, which often means a massive distortion or misinterpretation of what the author intended to say.

If a canon of literature is to be preserved in the colleges, and in the schools for that matter, of what ought the canon to consist? This question is no longer so easy to answer as it was in the nineteenth century or even the early twentieth century. But basically it ought to consist of literary works which have withstood the test of time. How much time? That too is not so easy a question to answer, but it may now be extended to include all but say the last half century. There is no such thing as an instant classic, especially in the school or university curriculum. A literary classic assumes and deserves an honored position, and not every literary work even from centuries ago can pass the test. One way of testing a literary classic might be what could be called the desert-island test. What 50 or 100 literary works would a highly educated person wish to take with him or her if it were necessary to spend 20 years on a desert island? Many of the works now taught in the colleges could never pass such a test, and some of the choices now seriously offered up for study in college literature classes would ludicrously fail to pass the desert-island test. Similarly many literary classics which would or should easily pass have disappeared from the university scene altogether and many more are in a fair way to follow.

*****

A no less ominous development in some college English departments of all sizes is the growing movement to abolish them entirely in favor of titles which encompass more than literature or language. There is now a tendency to rename them Departments of Cultural Arts or Interdisciplinary Arts or to bring them under the burgeoning mantle of Communications, or in other ways to de-emphasize the great literary achievements of our cultural heritage. If large English departments still teach the major poems, plays, and fiction of the Western world— and many of them still do—they may, with equal emphasis and enthusiasm, be teaching not only journalism and technical writing, but linguistics, Black studies, gender studies, third-world cultures, gay and lesbian studies, and even motion pictures, soap operas, the film, popular songs, and popular culture in general. These developments are certain to contribute to the destruction of any sort of literary canon, as English and literature departments in many colleges continue to lose their very identity.

It must be said too, however, that modern poets and dramatists and novelists have often not helped much to preserve the literary arts to which they contribute. The chief problem may be that many of them have done much to separate the writer from the reader by an increasing obscurantism which has become the hallmark of much modern, and especially contemporary literature, most notably in poetry. Many of even the best twentieth century poets have nurtured obscurantism, i.e., deliberate obscurity, which automatically cuts off a large portion of the literate public from the joys of poetry. T. S. Eliot has maintained that modern poetry "must be *difficult* [italics his] because of the variety and complexity of our civilization playing upon the fine sensibilities of the poet who must become more and more comprehensive, more allusive more indirect, in order to force, to dislocate if necessary language into his meaning." ["The Metaphysical Poets," *Selected Essays, 1917-32*, p.147] Eliot did not invent obscurantism in poetry, but by virtue of his genius he dignified it and his successors practiced it with a vengeance. On a more controversial note, it may be too that the pre-occupation of poets with free verse which eliminates the beauty of rhyme and stanzaic patterns and usually rhythms as well, has taken away much from the beauty of poetry. Free-verse poets have thus brought upon themselves the curse of unquotability and forgetability, and have thus made literary immortality more difficult for themselves. But the practice of free-verse poetry is so widespread that if Congress could outlaw it, the number of poets in the country would be diminished from upwards of 6 million to perhaps no more than a few thousand poets, or perhaps even a few hundred.

The fact that poetry has become one of the most unwanted commodities on the American market is attributable no doubt in part to the fact that students no longer read much of it in schools and colleges, but also to the fact that few readers care to invest money in most published poets' free-verse efforts.

Contemporary drama has also lost its staying power partly because of the dearth of first-rate dramatists and partly because many serious dramatists represent fashionable philosophical schools of despair, alienation, and various forms of nihilism, none of which make the spectator feel better after having seen one of their plays. But American audiences have also lost their appetite for legitimate theater partly no doubt on account of the pervasiveness of television, but partly too, because students at all levels of education get little exposure to the great plays of the world.

The only remaining genre of the literary arts is prose fiction, and it too has fallen upon hard times. The bottom has dropped out of the short story market, for those periodicals which at one time did much to perpetuate the genre are either defunct or now run far more heavily to non-fiction than fiction—another sign of the times—and the publication of collections of short stories has become increasingly rare in America. The serious novel still hangs on, but in a somewhat sickened condition, partly because of the lack of novelists of genius. Consummate craftsmanship in fiction has become increasingly rare in America, and with the exception of some spectacularly notable triumphs, the novel— even in Europe—particularly during the past half century, seems to be falling far short of the great novel tradition of the nineteenth century. The increasing preference for non-fiction over fiction and the relentless competition of audio-visual media have also cut deeply into the popularity of the serious novel, as has the weak literary education students get in both the schools and the colleges, such as I have been emphasizing in this study.

There is still another major reason to believe that the future of literature is not bright, and in a way it may be the most serious, at least the most sinister, namely the persistence of the belief that the scientific method, the authority of the senses, as opposed to the authority of the imagination, is the most reliable source of truth about the human condition. I have tried in the first chapter of this study to trace the rise of the supremacy of the scientific method in the nineteenth century and to suggest how thoroughly it has influenced not only critical theory but educational theory in the twentieth century, and how its influence has served to trivialize the importance of the literary arts. Furthermore, it is hard to envision a time when intellectuals, and hence eventually non-intellectuals, will once again reaffirm the authority of the written word in the form of literature, history, and philosophy— and religion— as the highest and most worthy source of truth about the human condition. The scientific spirit, including the behavioral scientific spirit, is fundamentally anti-humanistic and is liable to prevail for a long time to come. And as I have emphasized, it has infected every method of inquiry from the humanities themselves to the very language upon which the humanities, including literature, depend.

And finally given the unstoppable march of audio-visual and electronic technology, and all its dazzling attractions, there is increasing reason to believe that the joys and profits of literature will be increasingly confined to a tiny literary elite.

*****

But there is also plenty of evidence, after all these pessimistic prognostictions, that the written word, including serious literature, is a long way from dying out. One hopeful and crucial sign is that the attempted revolution in the teaching of reading in California with its move to throw out the patently unworkable "whole language" method in favor of a return to a phonics based reading program will spread to other states. California led the nation in introducing the "whole language" method, and it may very well lead the nation in abandoning it. In fact, other states have already begun to examine the reading failures in their schools and to entertain a return to a solidly basic phonics approach, for it was also the approach which was used in nineteenth and early twentieth century American schools and which enable students to read the high-quality literary texts of the McGuffey readers and other readers of roughly the same quality. Such a move could raise dramatically the level of literacy throughout the country. The resulting higher quality of the readings in elementary schools could thus also be raised in the middle schools and high schools with the consequent improvement of the literature studied there. It should be understood, however, that the restortion of phonics would meet with the resolute resistance of the entire educational establishment, which has been commited to a non-phonics approach to reading for more than half a century, and which is why reading reform must, however unpalatable, be carried out at the governmental, not the academic level.

There have also been concerted efforts among the schools at all levels in recent years to tighten up the curriculum by requiring students to be better prepared in all of the basic disciplines, but so far those efforts have been very mixed, and vast numbers of students are still allowed to graduate from high school without much knowledge of literature, history, geography, mathematics, the sciences, and of course, reading ability. But at least the direction is right.

At the university level organizations have now popped up which attempt to reverse the looseness of college curricula and to combat the massive move to politicize the humanities, including literature. The Association of Literary Scholars and Critcs (ALSC), for example, aims to restore the study of the humanities to their rightful place in the curriculum and to combat the destructive forces of current literary theories which depreciate the value of literature, such as I have described in this study, including the influence of deconstructionism and the wide variety of approaches to politicizing literature wihch are now current and which permeate the Modern Language Association.

The members of the ALSC number among them some of the most distiguished scholars and critics in the nation, and their numbers are growing rapidly both among older and younger scholars and critics. Another and even larger organization, the National Association of Scholars, which represents 3,500 academics serves as a kind of academic watchdog against the general deterioration of the core curriculum, and issues reports such as "The Dissolution of General Education: 1914-1993," already referred to in this study. And there are other individuals as well as organizations at work which suggest that all is not well in academia, so that there is now palpable evidence of widespread discontent in the academic world with the direction which many if not most colleges and universities are taking. Even parents are beginning to suspect that they are not getting their money's worth for what they pay to put their children through college.

There is no question too but that literacy will survive in this country, even if the study of the great literature has faded away. Full-blown literacy is everywhere still cherished as an ideal, indeed as a necessity, and there is still enough of it around to keep the wheels of an advanced society going. Reading is still taught in school, and many students who don't read well from their study in the classroom are helped at home or else are intelligent enough to figure out on their own the sounds of the letters and the words which they are not formally taught. And if high school graduates cannot read very well, a large percentage of them go on to college, after which many of them join the fully-literate club.

Furthermore, the number of books published in America is increasing, not decreasing, and is now approaching a 20 billion-dollar-a-year industry. According to the 1994 edition of the *Statistical Abstract of the United States,* Americans bought 2 billion books, 1.2 billion of them in paperback, with the 35-44 year age group buying more than any other. It is, of course, true that the vast majority of these are in the non-book tradition, like cookbooks, how-to books, tell-it-all books, and a host of other highly non-literary genres, and that the percentage of serious books, fiction or non-fiction has declined. High quality fiction, which is less and less available, has given way to low quality fiction, chiefly mysteries and romances, though even a few of these seem to have some genuine literary value.

Similarly, newspapers and periodicals are everywhere, though the number of big city daily newspapers is declining as are the number of intellectually demanding periodicals and journals of opinion. Special interest periodicals, however, continue to burgeon. Furthermore, it may be said that computers are doing much to keep the written word alive, since most computer programs and on-line services permit, indeed require, a fairly high degree of literacy or at least call for a certain skill in the written word. The point is, then, that the popularity and necessity of relying on the written word is not in imminent danger of collapse.

How much of that literate energy will be directed toward the best literature of this century or any other century is another question. All the evidence seems to suggest less and less. Light fiction still enjoys a considerable market and featherweight fiction an even greater market. What literature needs most desperately now if it is to survive is an enduring rationale, the kind of rationale which the literary theorists are not providing. The sterility of much literary scholarship is not providing it, which is chiefly why it is sterile. The destructors are out to destroy its authority entirely, and the increasingly dominant school which politicizes literature offers what can only be described as fraudulent in so far as it insists that literary works are above all political documents to be *used* in order to pursue political ends. Everybody who has read much of the greatest literature knows that it cannot be submitted to political scrutiny without being distorted, misinterpreted, and misused.

But if these groups of critical theorists are serving literature so badly then what kind of critical theory will serve it well? The answer would seem to be that only a return to the insistence upon the moral purpose of literature, as this study has attempted to demonstrate. Few perhaps are more aware than I that at the end of the twentieth century to insist upon the moral purpose of literature is not popular, even though, as we have seen, it was the fundametal premise of virtually all the literary theorists from Aristotle to Matthew Arnold, and in a few isolated instances beyond.

But the task of restoring the importance of the moral value of literature is far greater than it was for the great apologists for literature during the sixteenth, seventeenth, and eighteenth centuries, who had merely to rescue it from the hostility of the Platonists and the medieval Christian intellectuals, including the Church. As history has demonstrated, they succeeded. In the twentieth century, on the other hand, it may be that twenty Sir Philip Sidneys with twenty times his logic and rhetoric might not succeed. The case may well be hopeless. One might in fact suggest in all solemnity that the great literature has had its day, that it will in time be laughed out of existence not only by philosophers and scientists and the educational establishment and the businesss community, but the academic world itself.

On the technological level there is particular cause for alarm because there seems to be a vision of an electronic society in which the printed page is on its way out and that an electonic world can take care of whatever knowledge, emotional experience, and wisdom were formely stored up between the covers of great literature books. It is becoming generally regarded as a step that will advance civilization and that literature will in time become as outmoded as the quill pens which produed much of the best of it. Given that kind of atmosphere and that kind of expectation, the prospects for literature seem bleak.

But despite the daunting threats to literature which I have identified in this study and which prevail not only in America but to a lesser degree perhaps in other societies and around the world, there remains the consolation for some of knowing that literature still potentially retains the same moral and aesthetic powers that Sidney and Dennis and Samuel Johnson and Matthew Arnold and a host of other critics of the past, including a few from the twentieth century, have claimed for it. And these distinctive moral and social and aesthetic powers are still there to be tapped.

Meanwhile, the conclusion of this study may be said to bring both bad news and good news: the bad news is that literataure is dying as a consequential cultural force in America; the good news is that it is dying slowly.

Appendix

Literary Declarations:

A representative gathering of statements concerning the nature and purpose of literature from Plato to the present

The Classical Period

1. **PLATO:** The poet is "concerned with an inferior part of the soul; and therefore we shall be right in refusing to admit him into a well-ordered state, because he awakens and nourishes and strengthens the feelings and impairs the reason."—*The Republic*

2. **PLATO:** "Poetry feeds and waters the passions instead of drying them up; she lets them rule, although they ought to be controlled, if mankind are ever to increase in happiness and virtue."—*The Republic*

3. **PLATO:** "We must remain firm in our convictions that hymns to the gods and praises of famous men are the only poetry which ought to be admitted into our state."—*The Republic*

4. **ARISTOTLE:** "Tragedy, then, is an imitation of an action that is serious, complete, and of a certain magnitude; in language embellished with each kind of artistic ornament, the several kinds being found in separate parts of the play; in the form of action, not narrative, through pity and fear effecting the proper purgation or these emotions."—*The Poetics*

5. **ARISTOTLE:** "Poetry...is a more philosophical and a higher thing than history, for poetry tends to express the universal, history the particular."—*The Poetics*

6. **HORACE:** "The aim of the poet is to inform or delight, or to combine together, in what he says, both pleasure and applicability to life."—*The Art of Poetry*

7. **HORACE:** "As people avoid someone afflicted with the itch, with jaundice, the fits, or insanity, so sensible men stay clear of a mad poet; children tease him and rash fools follow him. Spewing out verses, he wanders off, with his head held high, like a fowler with his eyes on the blackbirds, and if he falls into a well or ditch he may call out, 'Help, fellow citizens!' but no one cares to help him."—*The Art of Poetry*

8. **LONGINUS:** "The effect of elevated language upon an audience is not persuasion but transport."—*Treatise on the Sublime*

The Medieval and Renaissance Periods

9. **DONATUS:** "Comedy is a story treating of various habits and customs of public affairs, from which one may learn what is of use in life, on the one hand, and what must be avoided, on the other."—*De Comaedia et Tragoedia*, 4th century

10. **SIR THOMAS ELYOT:** "Although I do not approve the lesson of wanton poets to be taught unto all children, yet I think it convenient and necessary that when the mind is become constant and courage is assuaged or that children of their natural disposition be shamefast and continent, none ancient poet would be excluded from the lesson of such one as desires to the perfection of wisdom."—*The Book Named the Governor*, 1530

11. **MINTURNO:** "The common purpose of all poets is, as Horace teaches, that of providing pleasure and profit."—*Arte Poetica*, c.1570

12. **SIR PHILIP SIDNEY:** "The ending end of all earthly learning [is] virtuous action."—*A Defence of Poesie,* c.1583

13. **SIR PHILIP SIDNEY:** "The philosopher...and the historian are they which would win the goal, the one by precept, the other by example. But both, not having both, do both halt....Now doth the peerless poet perform both; for whatsoever the philosopher says should be done, he giveth a perfect picture of it in some way by whom he supposeth it was done; so as he coupleth the general notion with the particular example. A perfect picture, I say, for he yieldeth to the powers of the mind an image of that whereof the philosopher bestoweth but a worthy description; which doth neither strike, pierce, nor possess the sight of the soul so much as that other doth [i.e., the poet]."—*A Defence of Poesie,* c.1583

14. **SIR PHILIP SIDNEY:** "No learning is so good as that which teacheth and moveth to virtue and that none can both teach and move thereto so much as Poetry, then is the conclusion manifest that ink and paper cannot be to a more profitable purpose employed."—*A Defence of Poesy,* c.1583

15. **GEORGE PUTTENHAM:** "Poetry deals with the praise of virtue and the reproof of vice, the instruction of moral doctrines, the revealing of sciences natural and other profitable arts, the redress of boisterous and sturdy courage by persuasion, the consolation and repose of temperate minds; finally, the common solace of mankind in all his travails and cares of this transitory life."—*The Art of English Poetry*, 1589

16. **SIR JOHN HARRINGTON:** "There be many good lessons to be learned out of it [poetry], many good examples to be found in it, many good uses to be had of it, and therefore it is not nor ought not to be despised by the wiser sort, but so to be studied and employed as was intended by the first writers and devisers thereof, which is to soften and polish the hard and rough dispositions of men and make them capable of virtue and good discipline."—*Preface to a Translation of Ariosto's* Orlando Furioso, 1591

17. **BEN JONSON:** "Poesy is the queen of arts, which had its origin from heaven, received it thence from the Hebrews and held in prime estimation with the Greeks, transmitted to the Latins and all nations that professed civility. The study of poetry (if we will trust Aristotle), offers to mankind a certain role and pattern of living well and happily; disposing us to all civil offices of society. If we will believe Tully [Cicero], it nourisheth and instructeth our youth; delights our age; adorns our prosperity ; comforts our adversity; entertains us at home; keeps us company abroad; travels with us; watches; divides the time of our earnest and sports; shares in our country recesses and recreations....Inasmuch as the wisest and best learned have thought her the absolute mistress of manners; and nearest of kin to virtue. And whereas they entitle philosophy to be a rigid and austere poesie, they have (on the contrary) stiled poesy a dulcet and gentle philosophy, which leads on and guides us by the hand to action with a ravishing delight and incredible sweetness."—*Timber or Discoveries,* c.1604

18. **MIGUEL DE CERVANTES:** "The spectator of a good drama is amused, admonished, and improved by what is diverting, affecting and moral in the representation; he is cautioned against deceit, corrected by example, incensed against vice, stimulated to the love of virtue. Such are the effects produced by dramatic excellence."—*Don Quixote*, 1605

19. FRANCIS BACON: "As for narrative poetry, or, if you please, heroical, so you understand it of the matter, not the verse, it seems to be raised altogether from a noble foundation, which makes much for the dignity of man's nature. For seeing the sensible world is in dignity inferior to the soul of man, poesy seems to endow human nature with that which history denies, and to give satisfaction to the mind, with at least the shadow of things, where the substance cannot be had. For if the matter be thoroughly considered, a strong argument may be drawn from poetry, that a more stately greatness of things, more perfect order, and a more beautiful variety delights the soul of man than can be any way found in nature since the Fall."—*The Advancement of Learning*,1605

20. JEAN CHAPELAIN: "Epic and dramatic poetry, which, having for its purpose the pleasure and profit of the auditors or the spectator, the epic or dramatic poet can the more surely encompass by making use of the natural, or verisimilar, rather than what is simply true or matter of fact, because it convinces men the more easily as it finds no resistance in them, which it would be if the poet adhered to mere facts, and which might well be so strange and incredible that they would think them false and refuse to be persuaded by them."—*Opinions of the French Academy on the Tragi-Comedy* The Cid, 1637

The Neo-Classical Period and the 18th Century

21. FRANCOIS HEDELIN, ABBÉ D'AUBIGNAC: "The stage ought to be instructive to the public by the knowledge of things represented; and I have always observed that it is not agreeable to an audience that man, who swerves from the way of virtue, should be set right and repent, by the strength of precepts and sentences: we rather desire it should be some advantage that presses him, and forces him to take up reasonable and virtuous sentiments."—*The Whole Art of the Stage*, 1657

22. PIERRE CORNEILLE: "It is impossible to please according to the rules without at the same time supplying a moral purpose of some sort."—*On the Uses and Elements of Dramatic Poetry*, 1662

23. **PIERRE CORNEILLE:** "...the punishment of wicked actions and the reward of good ones...is not an art precept but a custom which we have adopted, which one can abandon only at one's own risk,"— *On the Uses and Elements of Dramatic Poetry*, 1662

24. **JOHN DRYDEN:** "A play ought to be a just and lively image of human nature, representing its passions and humours and the changes of fortune to which it is subject, for the delight and instruction of mankind."—*An Essay of Dramatic Poesy,* 1668

25. **JEAN-BAPTISTE POQUELIN MOLIÈRE:** " If it be the aim of comedy to correct man's vices, then I do not see for what reason there should be a privileged class."—*Preface to* Tartuffe, 1669

26. **JOHN MILTON:** "Tragedy, as it was anciently composed, hath been ever held the gravest, moralest, and most profitable of all other poems."—*Preface to* Samson Agonistes, 1671

27. **SAINT-ÉVREMOND:** "In our tragedies we neither introduce any villain who is not detested, nor any hero who does not cause himself to be admired. With us, few crimes escape punishment and few virtues go off unrewarded. In short, by the good example we publicly represent in the theater, by the agreeable sentiments of love and admiration that are discretely interwoven with a rectified fear and pity, we are in a capacity of arriving to that perfection which Horace desires."—*Of Ancient and Modern Tragedy*, 1672

28. **JEAN RACINE:** "What I can say is that in no other of my plays have I given virtue so exalted a place as in this: the slightest evil is severely punished; the very thought of crime is made as horrible as the commission of it; the weaknesses of love itself are treated as veritable shortcomings; the passions are exhibited with the purpose of showing the disorder into which they lead us; vice is introduced in such wise as to make us detest it in all its horrible deformity. This should properly be the chief purpose of those who work for the public; this is what the ancients kept constantly in mind. Their plays were a veritable school where virtue was of no less importance than with the philosophers. Hence it was that Aristotle laid down the rules of dramatic poetry, and Socrates, the wisest of philosophers, did not disdain to speak of the

tragedies of Euripides. We should like our works to be as solid and full of useful instruction as those of antiquity."—*Preface to* Phaedra, 1677

29. **JOHN DENNIS:** "Poetry [is] the best and the noblest kind of writing. For all other writers are made by precept, and are formed by art; but the poet prevails by the force of nature; is excited by all that's powerful in humanity and is, sometimes, by a spirit not his own exalted to divinity ."—*The Usefulness of the Stage*, 1698

30. **JOHN DENNIS:** "The Christian religion contains the best, nay, the only means to bring men to eternal happiness, so for the making men happy even in this life, it surpasses all philosophy; but yet I confidently assert that if the stage were arrived to that degree of purity to which in the space of some little time it might easily be brought, the frequenting our theaters would advance religion and, consequently the happiness of mankind and so become a part of the Christian duty."— *The Usefulness of the Stage*, 1698

31. **JOHN DENNIS:** "The intention of poetry and the Christian religion, being alike to move the affections, they may very well be made instrumental to the advancing each other."—*Advancement and Reformation of Poetry*, 1701

32. **GEORGE FARQUHAR:** "*Utile dulce* was his [Aesop's] motto, and must be our business."—*A Discourse upon Comedy in Reference to the English Stage*, 1702

33. **JOHN DENNIS:** "The use of religion in poetry was absolutely necessary to raise it to the greatest exaltation of which so noble an art is capable, and on the other side that poetry was requisite to religion in order to its making more forcible impressions upon the minds of men."— *The Grounds of Criticism in Poetry*, 1704

34. **JOHN DENNIS:** "That poetry is miserably fallen, is, I suppose, granted, and, as there never was more occasion for a just and impartial criticism on account of the generality of writers; so, there never was more necessity for one on account of the readers and spectators. For the taste of both the readers and the spectators was never so debauched as it is at present....The design of [*The Grounds of Criticism of Poetry*]

is not only to retrieve so noble an art and to fix the rules both of writing and of judging, that both readers and writers may be at some certainty; but to raise it to a height which it has never known before among us, and to restore it...to all its greatness and to all its innocence."—*The Grounds of Criticism in Poetry*, 1704

35. **JOHN DENNIS:** "That poetry is the noblest of all arts, and by consequence the most instructive and most beneficial to mankind may be proved by the concording testimony of the greatest men who have lived in every age; the greatest statesmen, who have, as it were, unanimously cherished, esteemed, admired it, and never has it been disesteemed or neglected by any but some pretenders to wisdom, and by some contemptible politicasters, persons who have got into the management of affairs only by the weakness of those who have employed them, and who have utterly wanted capacity to know what a glorious use may be made of it for the benefit of civil society."—*The Grounds of Criticism in Poetry* , 1704

36. **JOSEPH ADDISON:** "As a perfect tragedy is the noblest production of human nature, so it is capable of giving the mind one of the most delightful and most improving entertainments."—*The Spectator, No.39*, 1711

37. **JOSEPH ADDISON:** "Words, when well chosen, have so great a force in them that a description often gives us more lively ideas than the sight of things themselves. The reader finds a scene drawn in stronger colors and painted more to the life in his imagination by the help of words than by an actual survey of the scene which they describe. In this case the poet seems to get the better of nature; he takes, indeed, the landscape after her, but gives it more vigorous touches, heightens its beauty and so enlivens the whole piece, so that the images which flow from the objects themselves appear weak and faint in comparison of those that come from the expressions."—*The Spectator, No. 41*, 1712

38. **VOLTAIRE:** "It [love on the stage] should either lead to misfortune and crime to convince us of its perils; or else virtue should triumph over it, to show that it is not invincible."—*A Discourse on Tragedy* , 1732

39. **SAMUEL JOHNSON:** "The design of tragedy is to instruct by moving the passions."—*The Rambler, No. 235*, 1751

40. **CARLO GOLDONI:** "Comedy was invented to correct the foibles and ridicule disagreeable habits: when the comedy of the ancients was written in this wise, the whole world liked it, for on seeing a facsimile of a character upon the boards, everybody saw the original either in himself or in some one else."—*The Comic Theater*, 1751

41. **SAMUEL JOHNSON:** "The business of a poet...is to examine, not the individual, but the species; to remark general properties and large appearances; he does not number the streaks of the tulip, or describe the different shades in the verdure of the forest. He is to exhibit in his portraits of nature such prominent and striking features as recall the original to every mind; and must neglect the minute discriminations, which one may have remarked, and another have neglected, for those characteristics which are alike obvious to vigilance and carelessness.

"But the knowledge of nature is only half the task of a poet; he must be acquainted likewise with all the modes of life. His character requires that he estimate the happiness and misery of every condition; observe the power of all the passions in all their combinations, and trace the changes of the human mind as they are modified by various institutions and accidental influences of climate or custom, from the sprightliness of infancy to the despondence of decrepitude. He must divest himself of the prejudices of his age or country; he must consider right and wrong in their abstract and invariable state; he must disregard present laws and opinions, and rise to general and transcendental truths, which will always be the same: he must therefore content himself with the slow progress of his name; contemn the applause of his own time, and commit his works to the justice of posterity . He must write as the interpreter of nature, and the legislator of mankind, and consider himself as presiding over the thought and manners of future generations; as a being superior to time and place.

"His labor is not yet at an end; he must know many languages and many sciences; and, by incessant practice familiarize to himself every delicacy of speech and grace of harmony."—*Rasselas*, 1759

42. **SAMUEL JOHNSON:** "The end of writing is to instruct; the end of poetry is to instruct by pleasing."—*Preface to Shakespeare*, 1765

43. **GOTTHOLD EPHRAIM LESSING:** "Comedy must only concern itself with such faults as can be remedied. Comedy is to do us good through laughter."—*The Hamburg Dramaturgy*, 1769

44. **CARLO GOLDONI:** "It was left to Molière to ennoble and render useful the comic stage in exposing the vices and laughable side of man to ridicule, for the purpose of correction."—*Memoirs*, 1795

45. **FREDRICH VON SCHILLER:** "The poetic spirit is immortal nor can it disappear from humanity; it can only disappear with humanity itself or with the aptitude to be a man, a human being—*On Simple and Sentimental Poetry* 1795

The Nineteenth Century

46. **WILLIAM WORDSWORTH:** "All good poetry is the spontaneous overflow of powerful feelings."—*Preface to* Lyrical Ballads," 1800

47. **WILLIAM WORDSWORTH:** "Poetry is the most philosophic of all writings...its object is truth, not individual and local, but general and operative; not standing upon external testimony, but carried alive into the heart of passion; truth which is its own testimony, which gives competence and confidence to the tribunal to which it appeals and receives them from the same tribunal. Poetry is the image of man and nature."—*Preface to* Lyrical Ballads, 1800

48. **WILLIAM WORDSWORTH:** "Poetry is the spontaneous overflow of powerful feelings; it takes its origin from emotion recollected in tranquillity; the emotion is contemplated till, by a species of reaction, the tranquillity gradually disappears, and an emotion, kindred to that which was before the subject of contemplation, is gradually produced, and does itself actually exist in the mind."—*Preface to* Lyrical Ballads, 1800.

49. **WILLIAM WORDSWORTH:** "A great poet...ought to a certain degree to rectify men's feelings, to give them new composition of feeling, to render their feelings more sane, pure, and permanent.—*Letter to John Wilson*, 1802

50. **WILLIAM HAZLITT:** "Poetry is the language of the imagination and the passions. It relates to whatever gives immediate pleasure or pain to the human mind. It comes home to the bosom and businesses of men; for nothing but what so comes home to them in the most general and intelligible shape can be a subject for poetry. Poetry is the universal language which the heart holds with nature and itself. He who has a contempt for poetry cannot have much respect for himself, or for anything else."—*On Poetry in General*, 1818

51. **JOHN KEATS:** "We hate poetry that has a palpable design upon us—and if we do not agree, seems to put its hand in its breeches pocket. Poetry should be great and unobtrusive, a thing which enters one's soul, and does not startle it or amaze it with itself, but with the subject."—*Letter*, 1818.

52. **PERCY SHELLEY:** "Poets are the unacknowledged legislators of the world."—*A Defence of Poetry*, 1821

53. **THOMAS LOVE PEACOCK:** The poet "lives in the days that are past....In whatever degree poetry is cultivated, it must necessarily be to the neglect of some branch of useful study, and it is a lamentable thing to see minds, capable of better things, running to seed in the specious indolence of the empty aimless mockeries of intellectual exertion. Poetry was the mental rattle that awakened the attention of intellect in the infancy of civil society, but for the maturity of mind to make a serious business of the playthings of childhood, is as absurd as for a grown man to rub his gum with coral, and cry to be charmed asleep by the jingle of silver bells."—*The Four Ages of Poetry*, 1820

54. **ROBERT SOUTHEY:** "Literature is not the business of a woman's life, and it cannot be."—*Letter to Charlotte Brontë*, 1837

55. **EDGAR ALLAN POE:** "I allude to the heresy of *The Didactic*. It has been assumed, tacitly and avowedly, directly and indirectly, that the ultimate object of all Poetry is Truth. Every poem, it is said, should inculcate a moral; and by this moral is the poetical merit of the work to be adjudged....We have taken it into our heads that to write a poem simply for the poem's sake, and to acknowledge such to have been our design, would be to confess ourselves radically wanting in the true Poetic dignity and force;—but the simple fact is, that, would we but permit ourselves to look into our souls, we should immediately

there discover that under the sun there neither exists nor *can* exist any work more thoroughly dignified—more supremely noble than this poem—this poem *per se*—this poem which is a poem and nothing more— this poem written solely for the poem's sake."—*The Poetic Principle*, 1848

56. **EDGAR ALLAN POE:** "I make Beauty the province of the poem, simply because it is an obvious rule of Art that effects should be made to spring as directly as possible from their causes;—no one as yet having been weak enough to deny that the peculiar elevation in question is at least *most readily* attainable in the poem. It by no means follows, however, that the incitements of Passion, or the precepts of Duty, or even the lessons of Truth, may not be introduced into a poem, and with advantage; for they may subserve, incidentally, in various ways, the general purpose of the work:—but the true artist will always contrive to tone them down in proper subjection to the *Beauty* which is the atmosphere and the real essence of the poem."—*The Poetic Principle*, 1648

57. **MATTHEW ARNOLD:** "Their [the poets'] business is not to praise their age, but to afford to the men who live in it the highest pleasure which they are capable of feeling." *Preface to Poems*, 1853

58. **GUSTAVE FLAUBERT:** "No great genius has come to final conclusions; no great book ever does, because humanity itself is forever on the march and can arrive at no goal. Homer comes to no conclusions, nor does Shakespeare, nor Goethe, nor even the Bible." *Letter to Mlle. De Chantepie*, 1857

59. **CHARLES BAUDELAIRE:** "There is another heresy, an error which has a more persistent life, I mean the heresy of didacticism, with its inevitable corollaries, the heresies of passion, truth, and morality. Most people assume that the object of poetry is some kind of teaching, that it must now fortify conscience, now perfect manners, now, in sum, demonstrate something useful. Poetry, however little one descends into oneself, integrates one's soul, recalls one's memories of enthusiasm, has no object but itself; it can have no other, and no poem will be so great, so noble, so truly worthy of the name of Poem as that which has been written solely for the pleasure of writing the poem.

I do not mean that poetry may not ennoble manners—let this be understood—or that its final result may not be to raise men above the level of common interests; that would be an obvious absurdity. I say that if the poet has pursued a moral end, he has diminished his poetical power; and it's not risky to say that his work will be poor. Poetry cannot, on pain of death or dethronement, be assimilated into science or morality; it does not have truth for its object but only itself. The means of demonstrating truths are altogether different."—*Theophile Gautier*, 1861

60. **MATTHEW ARNOLD:** "The critical power is of lower rank than the creative."—*The Function of Criticism at the Present Time*, 1864

61. **HIPPOLYTE TAINE:** "Herein lies the value of literary productions: they are instructive because they are beautiful; their usefulness increases with their perfection; and if they provide us with documents, it is because they are monuments. The more visible a book renders sentiments the more literary it is, for it is the special office of literature to take note of sentiments. The more important the sentiments noted in a book the higher its rank in literature, for it is by representing that sort of life a nation or an epic leads that a writer rallies to himself the sympathies of a nation or an epic. Hence, among the documents which bring before our eyes the sentiments of preceding generations, a literature and especially a great literature, is incomparably the best."—*Introduction, History of English Literature*, 1864

62. **FYODOR DOSTOEVSKY:** "I have my own idea about art, and it is this: what most people regard as fantastic and lacking in universality, I hold to be the inmost essence of truth. Arid observations of everyday trivialities I have long ceased to regard as realism—it is quite the reverse. In any newspaper one takes up, one comes across reports of wholly authentic facts, which nevertheless strike one as extraordinary. Our writers regard them as fantastic, and take no account of them; and yet they are the truth, for they are facts. But who troubles to observe, record, describe them? They happen every day and every moment; therefore they are not exceptional."—*Letter to Strakhan*, 1869

63. **WALTER PATER:** "Our one chance lies...in getting as many pulsations as possible into the given time. Great passions may give us

this quickened sense of life, ecstasy and sorrow of love, the various forms of enthusiastic activity, disinterested or otherwise, which comes naturally to so many of us.... Of this wisdom, the poetic passion, the desire of beauty, the love of art for art's sake, has most; for it comes to you professing frankly to give nothing but the highest quality to our moments as they pass, and simply for those moments' sake."—*Studies in the History of the Renaissance*, 1873

64. **MATTHEW ARNOLD:** "More and more mankind will discover that they have to turn to poetry to interpret life for us, to console us, to sustain us. Without poetry, our science will appear incomplete; and most of what now passes for religion and philosophy will be replaced by poetry; Science, I say, will appear incomplete without it....The day will come when we shall wonder at ourselves for having trusted to them [the sciences], for having taken them seriously; and the more we perceive their hollowness the more we shall prize the breath and finer spirit of knowledge offered to us by poetry."—*Introduction to* Ward's *English Poets*, 1880

65. **THOMAS HENRY HUXLEY:** "For the purpose of attaining real culture, an exclusively scientific education is at least as effectual as an exclusively literary education."—Quoted in Matthew Arnold's *Literature and Science*, 1882

66. **ANTON CHEKHOV:** "Human nature is imperfect, and it would, therefore, be strange to find only righteous people on this earth. But to think that the task of literature is to gather the pure grain from the muck heap, is to reject literature itself. Artistic literature is called so just because it depicts life as it really is. Its aim is truth—unconditional and honest."—*Letter to M.V. Kiselev*, 1887

67. **OSCAR WILDE:** "There is no such thing as a moral or an immoral book. Books are well written or badly written. That is all."—*Preface to* The Picture of Dorian Gray, 1891

68. **ÉMILE ZOLA:** "The masterpieces of modern fiction say more on the subject of man and nature than do the graver works of philosophy, history, and criticism. In them lies the modern tool."—*The Experimental Novel and Other Essays*, 1893

69. LEO TOLSTOY: "The business of art lies just in this—to make that understood and felt which, in the form of an argument might be incomprehensible and inaccessible. Usually it seems to be the recipient of a truly artistic impression that he knew the thing before but had been unable to express it."—*What is Art?* 1898

The Twentieth Century

70. T.S. ELIOT: "The business of the poet is not to find new emotions, but to use the ordinary ones, and in working them up into poetry, to express feelings which are not in actual emotions at all."—*Tradition and the Individual Talent*, 1917

71. IRVING BABBITT: "We should not hesitate to say that beauty loses most of its meaning when divorced from ethics even though every aesthete in the world would arise and denounce us as philistines."—*Rousseau and Romanticism*, 1919

72. IRVING BABBITT: "It is evident that the romantic ideal of art for art's sake means in the real world art for sensation's sake."—*Rousseau and Romanticism*, 1919

73. IRVING BABBITT: "One should insist...that the mark of genuinely ethical art, art that is highly serious, is that it is free from preaching."—*Rousseau and Romanticism*, 1919

74. T.S. ELIOT: "The only way of expressing emotion in the form of art is by finding an "objective correlative"; in other words, a set of objects, a situation, a chain of events which shall be the formula for that *particular* emotion; such that when the external facts, which must terminate in sensory experience, are given, the emotion is immediately evoked."—*"Hamlet,"* 1919

75. T.S. ELIOT: "It appears likely that poets in our civilization, as it exists at present, must be *difficult.* Our civilization comprehends great variety and complexity, playing upon a refined sensibility, and must therefore produce various and complex results. The poet must become more and more comprehensive, more allusive, more indirect, in order to force, to dislocate if necessary, language into his meaning."—*"The Metaphysical Poets,"* 1921

76. **EDMUND WILSON:** "Eliot and Valéry...still in the tradition of Poe, regarded a poem as a specialized machine for producing a certain kind of state. Eliot called poetry 'a superior amusement.'" *Is Verse a Dying Technique?*, 1928

77. **JOSEPH WOOD KRUTCH:** "No increased power of expression, no greater gift of words, could have transformed Ibsen into Shakespeare. The materials out of which the latter created his works—his conception of human dignity, his sense of the importance of human passions, his vision of the amplitude of life—simply did not and could not exist for Ibsen, as they did not and could not exist for his contemporaries. God and Man and Nature had all somehow dwindled in the course of the intervening centuries, not because the realistic creed of modern art led us to seek out mean people, but because this meanness of human life was somehow thrust upon us by the operation of that same process which led to the development of realistic theories of art by which our vision could be justified."—*The Modern Temper*, 1929

78. **I.A. RICHARDS:** "Most readers, and nearly all good readers, are very little disturbed by even a direct opposition between their own beliefs and the beliefs of the poet."—*Practical Criticism*, 1929

79. **T.S. ELIOT:** "Beyond a belief that poetry does something of importance or has something of importance to do, there does not seem to be much agreement. It is interesting that in our time, which has not produced any vast number of important poets, so many people—and there are many more—should be asking questions about poetry."—*The Modern Mind*, 1933

80. **I.A. RICHARDS:** "The business of the poet...is to give order and coherence, and so freedom, to a body of experience."—*Science and Poetry*, 1935

81. **YVOR WINTERS:** "Poetry...should offer a means of enriching one's awareness of human experience and of so rendering greater the possibility of intelligence in the course of future action; and it should offer likewise a means of inducing certain more or less constant habits of feeling, which should render greater the possibility of one's acting, in a future situation, in accordance with the finding of one's improved intelligence. It should, in other words, increase the intelligence and

strengthen the moral temper; these effects should naturally be carried over into action."—*In Defense of Reason,* 1937

82. **PAUL VALÉRY:** "A poet's function is not to experience the poetic state; that is a private affair. His function is to create it in others. The poet is recognized...by the simple fact that he causes his readers to become "inspired." Positively speaking, inspiration is a graceful attitude with which the reader endows the poet; the reader sees in us the transcendent merits of virtue and graces that developed in him. He seeks and finds in us the wondrous causes of his own wonder."—*Power and Abstract Thought,* 1938

83. **ARTHUR MILLER:** "I believe that the common man is as apt a subject for tragedy in its highest sense as kings are. On the face of it this ought to be obvious in the light of modern psychiatry, which bases its analysis upon classic formulations, such as the Oedipus and Orestes complexes, for instance, which were enacted by royal beings, but which apply to everyone in similar emotional situations....As a general rule, to which there may be exceptions unknown to me, I think the tragic feeling is evoked in us when we are in the presence of a character who is ready to lay down his own life, if need be, to secure one thing—his sense of personal dignity."—*The New York Times,* February 27, 1949

84. **YVOR WINTERS:** "I believe that a poem...is a statement in words about a human experience....In each work there is a content which is rationally apprehensible, and each work endeavors to communicate the emotion which is appropriate to a judgment, rational and emotional, of the experience—that is a complete moral judgment in so far as the work is successful."—*The Function of Criticism,* 1957

85. **KEITH F. McKEAN:** "One of the attempts to limit the critic's scope...is the relatively new idea that the critic should not mix ethics with art. The quarrel here is usually about the critic's function, for many who hold the view would agree that the censor or the minister may measure literature by moral standards, but they believe that the professional critic should keep his hands off because they feel that the morality of the art is really irrelevant to its worth. The persons who are inclined to take this view may range all the way from the scientific scholar to the basement beatnik and just about the only thing they can agree on is the position that one should consider the work separate

from its cause and its effects. They all try to understand or evaluate the work with what they feel is uniquely appropriate to the art. And ethical principles, they will agree, are somewhat inappropriate."—*The Moral Measure of Literature*, 1961

86. **CHRISTOPHER FRYE:** "No work of literature is better by virtue of what it says than any other work."—*The Well-Tempered Critic*, 1963

87. **WALTER SUTTON:** "A great deal of thought and many thousands of words have been expended on the subject of literature and morality, and the present time (any present time) calls for a few more."—*Modern American Criticism*, 1963

88. **DOUGLAS BUSH:** "Criticism has become less of an art than a grim industry or solemn priestcraft, and in the process has lost most of the infectious gusto that used to inspire amateur impressionism in less doggedly conscientious times....The great achievements of scholarship and criticism have their pathological side, and we seem to have encountered the law of diminishing returns."—*Literary History and Literary Criticism*, 1964

89. **GEORGES POULET:** "The transmutation through language of reality into a fictional equivalent has undeniable advantages. The universe of fiction is infinitely more elastic than the world of objective reality. It lends itself to any use; it yields with little resistance to the importunities of the mind. Moreover—and of all its benefits I find this the most appealing—this interior universe constituted by language does not seem radically opposed to the me who thinks it....The greatest advantage of literature is that I am persuaded by it that I am freed from my usual sense of incompatability between my consciousness and its objects."—*The Phenomenon of Reading*, 1969

90. **WOLFGANG ISER:** "The hero in the novel must be pictured and cannot be seen. With the novel the reader must use his imagination to synthesize the information given him, and so his perception is simultaneously richer and more private; with the film he is confined merely to physical perception, and so whatever he remembers of the world he had pictured is brutally canceled out."—*The Reading Process: A Phenomenological Approach*, 1974

91. JEAN PAUL SARTRE: "If literature is not everything, it is worth nothing. This is what I mean by 'commitment.' It wilts if it is reduced to innocence or to songs. If a written sentence does not reverberate at every level of man and society, then it makes no sense. What is the literature of an epoch but the epoch appropriated by its literature?"— *The Purpose of Writing*, 1974

92. JOHN GARDNER: "Morality is infinitely complex, too complex to be *knowable* and far too complex to be reduced to any code, which is why it is suitable matter for fiction, which deals in understanding, not knowledge."—*The Idea of Moral Criticism*, 1977

93. ELAINE SHOWALTER: "The feminist critique is essentially political and polemical, with theoretical affiliations to Marxist sociology and aesthetics."—*Toward a Feminist Poetics*, 1979

94. ELAINE SHOWALTER: "The new sciences of the text based on linguistics, computers, genetic structuralism, deconstructionism, neo-formalism and deformalism, affective stylistics and psychoaesthetics, have offered literary critics the opportunity to demonstrate that the work they do is as manly and aggressive as nuclear physics—not intuitive, expressive and feminine, but strenuous, rigorous, impersonal and virile....Literary science in its manic generation of difficult terminology, its establishment of seminars and institutes of post-graduate study, creates an elite core of specialists who spend more and more time mastering the theory, less and less time reading the books. We are moving towards a two-tiered system of "higher" and 'lower" criticism, the "higher" concerned with the "scientific" problems of form and structure, the "lower" concerned with the "humanistic" problems of content and interpretation. And these lower levels, it seems to me, are now taking on subtle gender identities, and assuming sexual polarity—hermeneutics and hismeneutics."—*Toward a Feminist Poetics*, 1979

95. SANDRA M. GILBERT: "If the pen is a metaphorical penis, with what organ can females generate texts?—*Literary Paternity*, 1980

96. RAYMOND FEDERMAN: "The primary focus of fiction in the future will be not to pretend any longer to pass for reality, for truth, or for beauty. Consequently, fiction will no longer be regarded as a mirror to life, as a pseudorealistic document that informs us about life, nor will it be judged on the basis of its social, moral, psychological, metaphorical, commercial value. Future fiction will seemingly be devoid of any meaning; it will be deliberately illogical, irrational, unrealistic, non-sequitur, and incoherent."—*Surfiction: Fiction Now and Tomorrow.* 1981

97. **TERRY EAGLETON:** "From Percy Bysshe Shelley to Norman N. Holland, literary theory has been indissoluably bound up with political beliefs and ideological values. Indeed literary theory is less an object of intellectual enquiry in its own right than a particular perspective in which to view the history of our time."—*Literary Theory: An Introduction,* 1983

98. **TZVETAN TODOROV:** "What I would hope without really believing it possible, is that this whole unfortunate episode of contemporary criticism be rapidly forgotten, in order that we might make a new departure from the former conception of criticism. The question, 'What does this text mean?' is a relevant one, and we must still try to answer it, without discarding any context—historical, structural or other—which can assist us in this task."—*All Against Humanity ,* TLS (October 4, 1985)

99. **ALLAN BLOOM:** "Comparative literature has now fallen largely into the hands of a group of professors who are influenced by the post-Sartrean generation of Parisian Heideggerians, in particular Derrida, Foucault, and Barthes. The school is called Deconstructionism, and it is the last, predictable stage in the suppression of reason and the denial of the possibility of truth in the name of philosophy. The interpreter's creative activity is more important than the text; there is no text, only interpretation. Thus the one thing most necessary for us, the knowledge of what these texts have to tell us, is turned over to the subjective, creative selves of these interpreters who say that there is both no text and no reality to which the text refers. A cheapened interpretation of Nietzsche liberates us from the objective interpretives of the texts that might have liberated us from our increasingly low and narrow horizon. Everything has tended to soften the demands made on us by the tradition; this simply dissolves it.

"The fad will pass, as it has already in Paris, but it appeals to the worst instincts and shows where our temptations lie."—*The Closing of the American Mind,* 1987

100. **LYNNE CHENEY**, (Former chairman of the National Endowment for the Humanities): "Scholars of literature have declared the death of the old canon [of literature] without making an effort to construct a new one. Literary theorists have declared that texts are about language rather than about life, and they have devoted their energy to showing that they are all meaningless. With few scholars willing to say that one work is more important than another, what reason is there for a teacher to make students read Charlotte Bronte instead of Judy Blume? With many voices saying that texts have no meaning, publishers have no reason to include literature in their textbooks."—"Defending the Beleaguered Humanities,"—*The Chronicle for Higher Education,* June 24, 1987, p. 38

101. **IRVING HOWE:** "Few aspects of recent literary life seem more important than the loss of faith, perhaps even interest, in the idea of the common reader. Most literary people now live and work in universities, and not many of these still write for the common reader. It sometimes seems almost as if that figure has been banished, at least in the academic literary world, as an irritant or intruder, the kind of obsolete person who still enjoys stories as stories and still supposes that characters bear some resemblance to human beings."—"The Treason of the Critics," in *The New Republic*, June 23, 1989, p.28

102. **JOHN SILBER:** "If one cannot be knowledgeable in all things, knowledge of Shakespeare may be, in the final analysis, more important than knowledge of calculus."—"The Alienation of the Humanities" in *Academic Questions,* Summer, 1989, p. 20

Index

About the Author

Arther Trace was born in Denver, Colorado, and received a B.A. in English from the University of Denver. He served for three years in the armed services during World War II, and upon his return to the United States he received an M.A. in English from Columbia University and a Ph.D. from Stanford University. He taught English at the University of Nebraska, Purdue University, and John Carroll University in University Heights, Ohio, before retiring to Fayetteville, Arkansas. He is married with two daughters, both with Ph.D's in English, and his wife, Gladys, a widely published poet, was an assistant professor of English before coming to Fayetteville.

Other books which the author has published include *What Ivan Knows That Johnny Doesn't*, *Reading Without Dick and Jane*, *The Future of Literature*, *Christianity and the Intellectuals*, and *The Furnace of Doubt: Dostoevsky and The Brothers Karamazov*. He is also the co-author of a freshman college English text *Preparatory Reading for Writing*; he has edited *The Open Court Basic Readers*, grades 1-3; and he has written some forty articles in periodicals ranging from *The Modern Language Journal* to *The Saturday Evening Post*.